D1596882

KENTUCKY WILDCATS

Where Have You Gone?

GREGG DOYEL

SP

SPORTS PUBLISHING L.L.C.

www.SportsPublishingLLC.com

ISBN: 1-58261-930-1

All interior photos: *Lexington Herald-Leader* (unless otherwise noted)

Publishers: Peter L. Bannon and Joseph J. Bannon Sr.
Senior managing editor: Susan M. Moyer
Acquisitions editor: John Humenik
Developmental editor: Doug Hoepker
Art director: K. Jeffrey Higgerson
Dust jacket design: Heidi Norsen
Project manager: Greg Hickman
Imaging: Dustin Hubbart
Photo editor: Erin Linden-Levy
Vice president of sales and marketing: Kevin King
Media and promotions managers: Courtney Hainline (regional),
    Randy Fouts (national), Maurey Williamson (print)

Printed in the United States of America

Sports Publishing L.L.C.
804 North Neil Street
Champaign, IL 61820

Phone: 1-877-424-2665
Fax: 217-363-2073
www.SportsPublishingLLC.com

For Dad

From the fourth row of Tad Smith Coliseum, rooting for John Stroud to whip up on Rick Robey, we never saw this book coming . . . did we?

CONTENTS

ACKNOWLEDGMENTS

Before issuing my thanks, I offer my condolences to the family of Bob Brannum, who was 78 when he died in February 2005, not long after speaking to me for his chapter in this book. Brannum was delightful and accommodating, as were almost every ex-Kentucky player and coach contacted for this book. Thanks for sharing your stories.

Thanks also to the University of Kentucky sports information staff, most notably Scott Stricklin, Mandy Polley, Joyce Sims and Susan Lax. Fine people, all of you.

I must also say thanks to web-based UK expert Jon Scott and his mountain of information (found at www.ukfans.net/jps/uk/wildcats.html); tireless politician Richie Farmer's equally tireless assistant, Gail Norris, a scary troll only on Halloween; *Lexington Herald-Leader* sports writer Jerry Tipton, whose Sunday column is a must-read for anyone with an interest in UK basketball; and ex-Vanderbilt player Perry Wallace.

Finally, thank you John Humenik, Doug Hoepker and the crew at Sports Publishing for the opportunity up front and the editing down the stretch; and to my boss at CBS SportsLine.com, Mark Swanson, for giving me time to pursue this project.

Where Have You Gone?

LAVON WILLIAMS

E very ex-Wildcat in this book has an interesting story to tell, but the author is allowed to have a favorite—and here he is.

Remember LaVon Williams?

What Williams did at Kentucky was splendid, playing on the 1978 national championship team and finishing his career with 726 points and 501 rebounds.

But what Williams has done since leaving Kentucky has been remarkable, starting with this boast that is undoubtedly true:

"As far as wood carving in the United States, I'm probably one of the best," he says. "Hands down, one of the best."

The Smithsonian agrees. So do various universities scattered around the South and Midwest. And so do collectors who routinely pay $5,000 for his carvings, which he describes as "urban American folk art."

"I might carve a jazz musician," Williams says. "It might be a scene from Kentucky. I do all sorts of carvings that deal with American life."

He must do it well, because art shows throughout the country clamor for his work. Williams's art has appeared in the 1992 Laurence Fishburne movie *Deep Cover* and as a logo for the Black Caucus of the American Library Association. His work also has run in university-sponsored museums and galleries at Ohio State, Morehead State, Kentucky and the University of Cincinnati. He is a staple of folk-art shows throughout the Southeast, and his work is regularly on display (and on sale) at The Art Exchange in Columbus, Ohio.

Ask him for his favorite exhibit, and Williams mentions one that debuted in December 2000 at the Smithsonian Institution in Washington

LaVON WILLIAMS

Years lettered: 1976-77, 1977-78, 1978-79, 1979-80
Career totals: 726 points, 501 rebounds, 66 assists, 18 blocks

D.C., called "When the Spirits Move: African American Dance in History and Art." For that exhibition, Williams carved a dancing scene he called "Rent Party."

A review of his work appeared in 2000 in the weekly newspaper *Cincinnati CityBeat*, which said Williams "collapses the dimension of depth in his painted wood carvings, compressing the life of his figures into intense, emotional lines. His pieces seem to reflect a cubist influence transposed into a warmer mood."

Williams is a fifth generation wood carver, a craft he began to learn at age 15 in Denver, Colorado. He also learned how to play basketball well enough to win Mr. Basketball for the region called the "State of Four Corners"—a reference not to Dean Smith's slowdown offense, but to the confluence of Colorado, Utah, Arizona and New Mexico.

That earned Williams a scholarship to Kentucky in 1976, and after two seasons as the team's ninth man—he averaged 1.9 points in 8.7 minutes as a sophomore on Kentucky's 1978 NCAA championship team—he was a starting forward as a junior and senior.

The Cleveland Cavaliers took Williams in the fifth round of the 1980 draft, but he didn't stick in the NBA. He did earn money playing basketball, though, first in Europe and then in Japan, before returning to the United States with no clear idea of what to do next.

"I just wanted a job back in the States, just wanted to get settled again," he says. "It's not as simple as it sounds, trying to get normal again after you've been playing basketball all your life."

Williams landed a job in commodities, trading them for four years on the Chicago Mercantile Exchange. That helped him decompress after his time in basketball, and it got him onto his feet in the United States, but it wasn't the career for him.

"It wore me out," he says. "I got tired of it. I like discipline, but a certain kind of discipline. That wasn't my personality; I was kind of out of my element. It wasn't what I had a passion for."

What he had a passion for was wood carving, and Williams began to hone his craft. Using his savings from professional basketball and the commodities market, Williams built his name in the art community. It wasn't easy, with Williams spending a day or two on a carving but then selling it for as little as $30.

Over time, Williams emerged as one of the premier carvers in this country and even abroad, getting invited to a handful of shows overseas. Now his carvings usually sell for somewhere between $2,000 and $5,000, though he still supplements his income by working as a mentoring counselor at a middle school in Lexington, Kentucky.

Williams's carving tools are simple: generally a pocketknife, mallet and a series of clamps and chisels. He brings them wherever he goes, which has led to some consternation at airports in the post-September 11 era of air travel. Williams no longer tries to carry his pocketknife on the plane, and he usually alerts airline officials to the unusual tools tucked away in his luggage.

"I tell them, 'I'm an artist—this is what I have,'" Williams says. "They'll look at it, and then it'll go under the plane."

As for raw materials, Williams needs a hunk of wood and he's ready to carve.

"I'm not one who can go look at a tree stump and say, 'I see people in it,'" he says. "I'm getting to that point, but most of the time I plan for the piece in advance."

Williams works on stumps or the occasional piece of wood that appears at his doorstep, left by a friend or fan who believes the wood to be just right for Williams's art. On his own, Williams scopes out area lumber mills for the right piece, usually settling on blocks of wood measuring two feet by three feet, though he has carved pieces much bigger.

One of his largest pieces was "Rent Party," which started as a rectangle measuring four feet by six feet. By the time Williams was finished, "Rent Party" had emerged—measuring nine inches by 51 inches—as a two-sided depiction of people dancing. That's a layman's description, anyway. Here's what Williams has had to say about his art:

"If you're trying to make a woman, you're not trying to do the most beautiful woman in the world," he says. "You're probably trying to express the soul or the inner part or the personality of a person, more so than trying to capture the exact image, like a photograph would do. You want to try to be as expressive as possible, as explosive as possible. You're looking for a fantastic movement or a fantastic shape that comes in the piece, and that's the whole power to the piece. You want it to explode out when the viewer sees it or you want it to be calm, but yet you still want a powerful presence in the piece, so that it dominates or takes off."

Williams advises a handful of young wood carvers, but he isn't sure there will be a sixth-generation carver in his family. He and his wife, former Kentucky women's star Debra Oden, have two daughters. Both of them are aspiring artists, Williams says, but neither has shown a consistent interest in carving.

"I have people who come by weekly to learn. Wood carving is being passed on," Williams says. "It just might not be passed on to my daughters."

Where Have You Gone?

DERON
FELDHAUS

When Deron Feldhaus left miniature Maysville for the University of Kentucky in 1987, he figured he'd left for good.

Maysville had been good to him, really good, but Maysville only had a population of 8,993 people—and basketball was going to give him the world. And it did. After becoming one of the more popular players in Wildcats lore, Feldhaus played several years in Japan. When his playing career was finished he returned to Lexington in the late 1990s to start the next phase of his life, whatever that phase might be, but darned if he didn't find himself going back to Maysville almost every weekend.

See, his father had a golf course, and Deron Feldhaus always did love to play golf. His father was getting older, too, and needed some help running the business. Deron was nothing if not a good son and ... oh, let's be honest, he missed Maysville. He missed it a lot. After a year in Lexington, he moved back to the miniature town of 8,993—make that 8,994.

"At the time Lexington was growing so much, the traffic was getting so bad, I was happy to go back to Maysville," Feldhaus says. "The one thing was, when I moved back to Maysville, I thought there was no way I'd get married there."

True. Maysville was too small. What were the odds of finding a woman—the right woman—in a town that small? It wasn't going to happen. On the other hand, Deron Feldhaus, meet Amy Huber.

"It really did work out perfect," says Deron. "I met my wife in Maysville and everything."

Deron and Amy Feldhaus are one of those couples who lived parallel lives before finally coming to an intersection. Like Deron, Amy grew up in

DERON FELDHAUS

Years lettered: 1988-89, 1989-90, 1990-91, 1991-92
Honors: retired jersey No. 12
Career totals: 1,232 points (29th in UK history), 540 rebounds,
217 assists, 98 steals

Maysville and attended the University of Kentucky. Like Deron, Amy returned to Maysville to work for the family business, in her case a construction company. It was during their second tours of Maysville that they finally met. They were married within a few years.

By then Feldhaus had bought into his family's business, Kenton Station Golf Course, one of three courses in Maysville. Deron was quite the golfer at Mason County High, tying for second in the state tournament as a senior in 1987, and working at Kenton Station has helped him bring his game back down to scratch. On the familiar courses around Maysville he's probably better than scratch, which makes him a leading contender in the area's big tournaments, like the Mason County Open and the Chippeways match play championship. In June 2004, Feldhaus finished second in the 69th annual Chippeways to a University of Kentucky golfer, Mark Blakefield, who beat the ex-Wildcats great three and two.

Make no mistake: Feldhaus is an ex-Kentucky great, even though his legacy has been (unfairly) tied closely to "The Shot," Duke forward Christian Laettner's infamous buzzer-beater over Feldhaus and John Pelphrey in the East Region championship of the 1993 NCAA Tournament. Feldhaus is reminded of that shot constantly, but never more often than in the spring when Kenton Station's clubhouse television is turned to March Madness and Laettner's shot comes on the tube.

"I say, 'There it is again, boys,'" Feldhaus says. "I don't watch it, I just turn my head. But I got over it quick. It was just one of those things. That game, it seems like everything spectacular was going to happen."

That it happened to Feldhaus has helped to obscure the fact that his career was much bigger than one shot. In its November 2002 rankings of the top 100 players in Kentucky history, the Louisville *Courier-Journal* ranked Feldhaus No. 85.

Feldhaus graduated in 1992 with 1,232 points, 540 rebounds and 217 assists. Those are solid numbers, but his contribution to Kentucky basketball can't be measured just by the numbers. Feldhaus joined seniors Pelphrey, Sean Woods and Richie Farmer to form the foundation of Kentucky's "Unforgettables" in 1991-92. They were the bridge from Eddie Sutton's rocky ending to Rick Pitino's solid start to the national dominance that followed in the mid-1990s.

Feldhaus was exceptionally team-oriented, taking a redshirt year during his first season on campus and offering to give up his scholarship during his final year.

"It didn't happen, but I offered to give it up because we were needing a scholarship, and Coach Pitino thought he might get another big-time player," Feldhaus says. "He asked me if I would give mine up, and I said yes. Anything to help the team."

Feldhaus already had done plenty of that. He averaged 14.4 points as a sophomore in 1990, but the arrival of Jamal Mashburn saw Feldhaus's playing time plummet from 34 minutes per game as a sophomore to 22 minutes as a junior. His scoring average also dropped, to 10.8 points per game as a junior and 11.4 per game as a senior, but as a team the Wildcats were getting better. After going a combined 27-33 in Feldhaus's redshirt freshman and sophomore seasons, the Wildcats went 51-13 in his final two years.

During Pitino's first season at Kentucky in 1989-90, he allowed a coach from Japan to observe practices and take what he had learned back to the professional leagues in Japan. The visiting coach did just that—and took Feldhaus with him. That came four years later, after Feldhaus had graduated, and Feldhaus enjoyed a five-year career overseas. He wanted to make it six, but it wasn't to be.

"They fired my coach, and because I was one of his guys, they fired me," Feldhaus says. "I wanted to stay one more year and I was [going to be] through. We started in the bottom division, Division Three. My last year we won Division Two, and I got fired. I wanted to play one more year in Division One and I was going to call it quits. I was real close to my family and friends, and being over there seven months was tough. I was getting ready to go back when I got my [dismissal] letter. That threw me for a loop. I just pondered on it, and decided that was the best thing."

Staying in Japan would have meant more time with basketball, but less time with golf. Feldhaus figures he played three times in all those years in Japan, and he paid handsomely to play at all.

"I didn't even take my clubs because it was so expensive over there," he says. "The cheapest round I played there was $150 or so. I had a couple of Japanese teammates who played, and we had to get tee times two months in advance. We'd go to the driving range, and even that was expensive. Some places in Tokyo, you have to have memberships for a driving range."

Membership to a driving range? That's ridiculous. Feldhaus's father, former Kentucky player Allen "The Horse" Feldhaus, was part owner of Kenton Station, and there was a standing offer for Deron to buy into the club when he was ready.

After trying to get his post-basketball bearings for a year in Lexington, Feldhaus was ready. He bought into Kenton Station, moved back home and unexpectedly met his wife. Now you couldn't pry Deron Feldhaus away from miniature Maysville. As far as he's concerned, Maysville is just the right size.

"This is home," Feldhaus says. "This is family."

Where Have You Gone?

MIKE CASEY

If you can believe it, Mike Casey isn't bitter. He's not angry, frustrated, any of that stuff.

But he could be.

Maybe he even should be.

Life has been good to Casey since the car crash that nearly killed him in 1969, including his plans for an early retirement at age 56, and that's why he can honestly look back on his basketball career—what it was and what it could have been, knowing there was a vast distance between the two—without rancor.

"You try to keep it in perspective," he says. "In any sport only the top one percent of the athletes make it to the top. I had a good run."

He had a *great* run, as did Kentucky, but for both of them it could have been better. Casey was a six-foot-four shooting guard from Shelbyville who had led Shelby County High to the state championship and won Kentucky's Mr. Basketball in 1966. He was a winner, plain and simple, and that continued at Kentucky, where he set a school record with 28 points in his varsity debut in 1968 and averaged 20 points that season to lead the team. He averaged 19.1 points the following season as a junior, deferring to teammate Dan Issel's rising star. Kentucky went a combined 45-10 in those two seasons but didn't reach the Final Four either year, a problem that figured to be rectified in 1969-70.

In all the years of Kentucky basketball, a program that has won seven national championships, it's possible the Wildcats have never been more promising than the summer before that 1969-70 season. Issel, Casey and Mike Pratt, who had averaged a combined 62.6 points in 1968-69, were all

MIKE CASEY

Years lettered: 1967-68, 1969-70, 1970-71
Honors: All-SEC 1967-68, 1968-69, 1970-71
Career totals: 1,535 points (11th in UK history),
558 rebounds, 260 assists

coming back as seniors. Issel, a center, was perhaps the best player in the country. Casey was an All-America candidate at guard. And if Pratt, a first-team All-SEC forward the previous season, was the third-best player on the team … well, that was going to be one unbelievable team.

But that summer, something truly unbelievable happened.

Mike Casey almost died.

It was a car crash. Casey was driving into Lexington from his parents' home in Simpsonville for some pickup basketball when his car went into a curve and blew a tire. The car spun around and rammed into a bar of concrete that was holding a utility pole.

A friend sitting next to Casey suffered scrapes and bruises, but Casey wasn't nearly as lucky. The pole broke off and went into the car, spearing Casey in the left leg, snapping the tibia and fibula in two. It could have been worse—the pole could have hit much higher up Casey's body—but the damage to his leg was severe. Both bones were sticking through the skin. Casey can still see it.

"My leg was bent back 90 degrees," Casey says. "I could feel it, and I could see the whole thing because I was [wearing] shorts. They had to cut me out of the car."

Casey was in the hospital nearly two weeks, and while he knew his injuries were serious, he had no idea they were career-threatening until a reporter from New York City called his hospital room.

"I don't know how he found out, but he called me from New York and was telling me how bad it was," Casey says. "Nobody had told me yet, but some of that was because I'd been pretty heavily sedated."

Kentucky coach Adolph Rupp was at a coaches' conference in New York when he learned the news from a Kentucky athletic department official. It's possible Rupp had to be sedated as well, though the record only shows that Rupp's first words were, "Well, there goes the national championship."

Probably so, yes. Casey redshirted the 1969-70 season, but Kentucky basketball carried on and even thrived, taking a 25-1 record and the No. 1 national ranking into the 1970 NCAA Tournament. The Wildcats were eliminated in the second round by Jacksonville, however, and it's not hard to wonder how that game, and that season, would have turned out with Casey as a blue shirt, not a redshirt.

Casey returned to Kentucky in 1970-71, but it wasn't the same. For one thing, Issel and Pratt had graduated. For another, Casey's left leg wasn't quite 100 percent, depriving him of his trademark first step. Casey would average 17 points per game that season, but people who saw him as a sophomore and junior said it was a different Mike Casey—a less explosive Mike Casey—who returned from that car crash.

Still, the ABA and the NBA were intrigued. Because of his redshirt season, Casey was eligible for the 1970 draft and then again after his senior season in 1971. All told he was selected by three teams: Chicago (in 1970) and Cleveland (1971) of the NBA, and Kentucky (1970) of the ABA. Casey says his agent negotiated a $125,000 contract with the nearby Kentucky Colonels, but it wasn't guaranteed. First, Casey would have to make the team. As camp wore down, Casey says the final roster spot came down to a competition between him and a rookie from Elizabeth City State named Mike Gale.

"His contract was going to be for something like $17,500, and mine was $125,000," Casey says. "It was a business decision. It got down to dollars and cents, and I got cut."

Not finished with basketball just yet, and still an amateur, Casey joined an AAU team that toured Europe. Averaging 27 points per game on that tour earned Casey an invitation to Colorado Springs, Colorado, to try out for the 1972 U.S. Olympic team. As had happened four years earlier, when he was cut at tryouts for the 1968 U.S. Olympic team in Phoenix after his sophomore season at Kentucky, it was not to be.

"I was third alternate [in 1972]," Casey says. "I scored, but Coach Iba [former Oklahoma State coach Henry Iba] was the U.S. coach and he didn't like offense—he loved defense. So I didn't make it."

Casey's AAU team had beaten the Russian national team twice in three tries. That same Russian team upset the Americans in the 1972 Olympics, one of the most memorable—and controversial—games in U.S. sporting history. Casey would have liked to have been a part of that one.

"It might have opened some doors," he says.

Casey had one more tryout left in him, but like the previous two, this one didn't work out. He says he was the last player cut from the ABA's Memphis Tams, and that was it. The great Mike Casey, whose sophomore season portended one of the great futures in Kentucky basketball, was finished at age 24.

Here's the beguiling thing about Casey: He didn't mope, didn't point fingers, didn't woe-is-me his way through the rest of the 1970s.

He barely stopped to catch his breath.

"I hung up my sneakers," Casey says. "It was time to go to work."

His first job was helping to work the family farm in Simpsonville, Kentucky. and after a few years of that he worked as an administrator in an area nursing home. From there he took a job in sales with Texo, a Cincinnati-based, industrial-chemical company founded by former Dallas Cowboys executive Tex Schramm. His region was roughly one-third of the state of Kentucky, which dovetailed nicely into his next job, with L.G. Balfour, selling school memorabilia such as class rings, caps and gowns.

By late 2004, Casey was planning to sell his Balfour territory, which had doubled in his 15 years with the company, and put the proceeds toward an early retirement. His region with Balfour had been roughly one-fifth of Kentucky, which he says led to almost 50,000 miles per year in the car and has translated to nearly 75,000 rings sold.

Some of those rings went to Kentucky in 1996 for its national championship.

The irony is so thick, you could cut it with a utility pole. Mike Casey, whose injury might have cost Kentucky the national championship in 1970, sold the school its NCAA title rings in 1996.

The story doesn't end in irony but in happiness. When he ordered the rings, then-Kentucky coach Rick Pitino ordered an extra ring.

Guess who got it?

The ring salesman. Mike Casey has his NCAA title ring after all.

Where Have You Gone?

DIRK MINNIEFIELD

In the late 1980s and early 1990s Dirk Minniefield spent more than 450 consecutive days in the Lexington County Jail—but he can tell you the exact day he hit rock bottom. He can tell you, and he can tell you with happiness and not sorrow in his voice, because that was also the day his life began to rocket in the right direction.

"It was the day my Mom came to visit me—the only time she came to visit me," Minniefield said. "That same day my Dad came down from Ohio, and my sons had been there earlier that day. I cried all day, and I knew this was not the place for me. This wasn't how the story was supposed to end."

Minniefield couldn't take an eraser to his past—to the cocaine addiction that claimed his NBA career, to the series of non-violent misdemeanors he committed while in the throes of that addiction—but he could damn sure start working on a better future. That day, in jail, Minniefield decided his days of abusing drugs and alcohol were finished.

"I had a celebrated childhood in Kentucky," Minniefield says. "When I was 12, I was considered one of the best players in the state by *Street and Smith* [magazine]. What I did on the basketball floor was always talked about, and here I am in jail? At that moment I made my mind up: When I get out, I'm going to do what I have to do to get myself clean."

More than a decade later, Minniefield has made good on that vow. Better than that, even. He has worked for the NBA Players Association since 1993 as something of a crisis counselor, mentoring players on the dangers that face them and serving as an adviser when a player's personal life veers in the wrong direction.

For the most part Minniefield can't specify which players he has helped, but put it like this: Think of any off-court incident involving an NBA play-

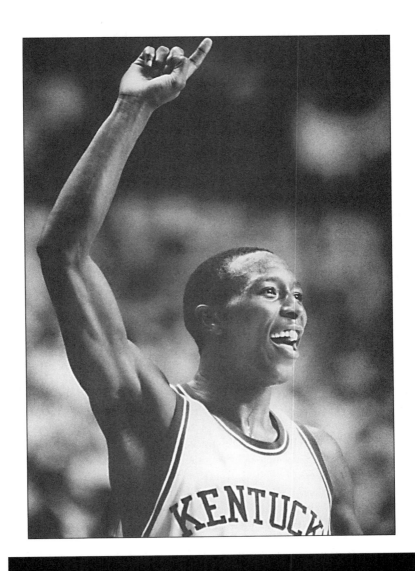

DIRK MINNIEFIELD

Years lettered: 1979-80, 1980-81, 1981-82, 1982-83
Career totals: 1,069 points (42nd in UK history), 331 rebounds,
646 assists (1st in UK history), 156 steals

er—any of them. Has Minniefield been involved behind the scenes, trying to help the player through that crisis? The odds are good, yes.

In today's business lexicon, Minniefield deals in the CI, or critical incident, phase of NBA life.

"What's a CI?" he says. "Say there's a domestic violence situation. I come in and counsel both individuals, and try to get to the root of the issue that caused the critical incident. I take that situation and help them work through it. I also work with drugs and substance abuse, because that's what my background stems from. I also work with anger management. I can talk about some of the guys I've worked with, guys whose issues have been well documented. Guys like Roy Tarpley, Richard Dumas, Shawn Kemp. Pretty much, those are the guys that have had incidents where they demanded one-on-one attention, and that's what I do."

Minniefield says every player in the NBA has his cellular phone number—every last one of them—but he doesn't do his work alone. His partner is Cliff Robinson (the retired NBA forward from Southern Cal, not the active NBA forward from Connecticut), and together they serve as mentors, counselors, big brothers.

To get where he has gotten today, Minniefield couldn't have done it by himself—and doesn't pretend he did. First and foremost, he credits God with turning his life around. Second, Minniefield says another former NBA player, recovered addict John Lucas, led him onto the proper path.

Minniefield and Lucas had much in common, much deeper than the No. 10 jersey each wore once upon a time for the Houston Rockets. Both were high school All-America point guards and high-profile college stars, and both saw their NBA careers sidetracked by addiction. Lucas fought off his demons several years before Minniefield first encountered his own, and by the time Minniefield knew he needed help, he also knew where to go for that help: John Lucas.

"He's done a lot for a lot of people who were in my situation," Minniefield says. "He was a good friend, so I sought him out. I went out there [to Lucas's rehab clinic in Houston] and got sober, and then I did some work for him [with Lucas's Miami Tropics of the United States Basketball League]. In the process of working for John Lucas, I obtained certification as a chemical dependency counselor. The job came open with the league, and I took on the job."

That was 1993, and Minniefield was certainly prepared. He already had performed nearly 4,500 hours of counseling work, volunteered in a Houston-area service called Bouncing Back and re-entered the mainstream as an assistant high school basketball and volleyball coach. With Bouncing Back, Minniefield joined forces with other ex-addicts like former ABA stars

Marvin Barnes and Gus Gerard, going to schools and businesses to speak about the dangers of addiction and the joy of recovery.

There is joy for Minniefield now, make no mistake about that. The shame, the guilt, the self-loathing—he felt all of those things, too, but that season has passed. It had to pass, he says, or there could have been no recovery.

"Most people have probably forgotten what I went through, but I don't hide it," he says. "I talk about it because I'm past the humiliation of it. I dealt with my demons. I came from a pretty rough neighborhood there in Lexington, but I don't blame anybody for what happened to me. Nobody put a gun to my head. I made some bad decisions and I suffered for them, and people around me suffered. My kids have had their own problems because of what I went through. That's the problem with the disease of addiction: it affects everybody who comes into contact with people who are addicted. Because of the things I did, I'm responsible for a lot of other people's misery as well as my own. That's something I've got to live with. It's been hard, but I'm okay with it today."

Today Minniefield derives his greatest pleasure from helping other players avoid the pitfalls that claimed his once-promising NBA career. Minniefield's addiction came after he had spent two years in the Continental Basketball Association and three years as an NBA journeyman, bouncing from Cleveland to Houston to Boston. With the Celtics, he looked to be on the verge of breaking out before his addiction took over.

Minniefield doesn't want that to happen to any of today's players. One of his favorites is Damon Stoudamire, whose career was in danger after three marijuana-related arrests in the previous 18 months caused his production to drop from 13.5 points and 6.5 assists per game in 2001-02 to 6.9 points and 3.5 assists in 2002-03. With help from Minniefield, Stoudamire got his production back to where it belongs in 2003-04, up to 13.4 points and 6.1 assists.

"Damon Stoudamire is like a poster child for me," Minniefield says. "He's turned his life around, matured, stepped up to the plate. He said, 'I made some mistakes, some bad choices, but hey—I'm doing something about it. This is who I am.' When I see that, knowing I had a hand in putting him on the right path, it makes me feel great.

"I could be doing a lot of things. I could probably be making a lot more money, but I'm at peace with myself. My family's taken care of, and I'm happy with what I do. When I see a guy make it back on the floor and he's being productive and he's matured to the point where he can deal with society … that's all I do, is help put them on the path. God does the rest. I'm just the guy who's there, trying to walk with them."

Players should listen to him. Dirk Minniefield already has walked miles in their shoes.

LOU TSIOROPOULOS

L ou Tsioropoulos's father was a foreman in a tannery, a brutal job in any era but an especially punishing form of employment in the 1950s. His father would come home beaten some days, almost broken others, which is why Tsioropoulos took his education at the University of Kentucky so seriously. He wanted to make sure he never had to spend a day in a tannery. He didn't, and in a minute you'll see how that Kentucky education took Tsioropoulos to the top of his field.

First, though, understand the irony here: It was that pursuit of education by Tsioropoulos—and two teammates—that cost Kentucky a spot in the 1954 NCAA Tournament.

The Wildcats clearly had the best team in the country in 1953-54, a 25-0 marvel led by the "Big Three" of Cliff Hagan, Frank Ramsey and Tsioropoulos. But because those three had all received their bachelor's degrees, they were ruled ineligible for postseason play. At the time, the NCAA Tournament didn't allow post-graduate students to compete in the tournament. Tsioropoulos, Hagan and Ramsey were unaware of that rule and had earned their bachelor's by January thanks to their extra year of schooling. (Kentucky hadn't fielded a varsity team in 1952-53 as punishment from the NCAA because of a point-shaving scandal during the late 1940s.)

As champion of the Southeastern Conference, Kentucky was more than welcome to represent the SEC in the 1954 NCAA Tournament, but the Wildcats would have to do so without the Big Three, who had produced nearly 60 percent of the team's points. Hagan averaged 24 points per game, Ramsey 19.6 and Tsioropoulos 14.5.

Photo courtesy of Linville Puckett

LOU TSIOROPOULOS

Years lettered: 1950-51, 1951-52, 1953-54
Honors: retired jersey No. 16
Career totals: 709 points, 699 rebounds, 73 assists

The team put it to a vote, and by a 9-3 tally the rest of the Wildcats decided to compete. Not so fast, Tsioropoulos said.

"I said, 'There will be no voting because you guys are not going,'" Tsioropoulos says. "We had done most of the scoring! Without us, that wouldn't have been the Kentucky team that won all those games."

Kentucky coach Adolph Rupp agreed, and the Wildcats stayed home. More than a half-century later they remain the only Division I team to finish a season undefeated yet not be recognized as the national champion. La Salle won the NCAA title that season by defeating Bradley in the championship game, but let the record show that Kentucky had smothered that same La Salle team, 73-60, that December in the UK Invitation Tournament.

That's irony.

But so is this: Tsioropoulos's pursuit of education may have cost him the end to his college career, but it also provided the foundation for a three-decade professional career in which he climbed to the top rung of his ladder.

Tsioropoulos became a high school coach and teacher. Then a counselor. Then an assistant principal. Finally, he became a principal. All of that happened in Louisville, where Tsioropoulos still has a home. He also has a home in Florida.

Education wasn't so bad for Tsioropoulos after all, was it?

"I've worn different hats, and I've loved them all," he says of his 1964-1995 tenure in education. "I was fortunate to have a lot of variety in my career."

Tsioropoulos has had a lot of variety in a lot of areas. He has multiple homes, he has had multiple nicknames, and he even had multiple weddings—to the same woman.

The homes, you know about: one in Louisville, one in Clearwater, Florida.

The nicknames? It's funny how that goes. As it turns out, Tsioropoulos has had nickname after nickname thrust upon him, the monikers forming layers that have obscured the fact that his given name is Elias. In the late 1940s, before people worried about such a thing as political correctness, Tsioropoulos says Greek people often were referred to as Louie, or Lou. That's how Elias Tsioropoulos became known as Lou Tsioropoulos, even if Lou (or Louie or Louis) is listed nowhere on his birth certificate.

"A lot of Greek guys where I came from, they called them Louie," Tsioropoulos says. "My wife doesn't like it."

Tsioropoulos also was called Plato, another Greek reference, before being tabbed by the media as "The Golden Greek." Tsioropoulos bristles at that for many reasons, including the fact that he was nowhere close to being "golden." He had dark hair and light skin. Golden Greek? Whatever.

"Every Greek guy, they say he's 'the Golden Greek,'" Tsioropoulos says. "My teammates didn't call me that. I didn't need a nickname. My last name was enough to identify me."

In August of 1963 he introduced himself as Lou Tsioropoulos to the pretty sister of a neighbor in Louisville. Within three weeks, they were engaged. On May 16, 1964, Lou and Jan Tsioropoulos were married at a protestant church in Louisville.

"The Greek people didn't like that," Tsioropoulos says. "We were married at an Episcopal church, and I think they were ready to excommunicate me back home. So in August we flew to Massachusetts and got married at a Greek church. We had a small wedding up there."

Tsioropoulos had been raised in Lynn, Massachussetts, so imagine his excitement to be drafted by the nearby Boston Celtics. It was a dream come true for the former star at Classic High in Lynn, but it was also a dream deferred. First came the Korean War. Tsioropoulos had been drafted into the Air Force earlier, while still at Kentucky, and had been commissioned as a second lieutenant before his final season. He was a member of the reserves in 1953-54, then embarked on his two-year military stint later that summer.

Luckily for Tsioropoulos, the Korean War had ended the year before—after he was drafted, but before he served—so his service was highlighted by football and basketball. He was an All-Air Force halfback based in Dover, Delaware, and when he transferred to Andrews Air Force Base in Maryland, he was reunited with Hagan. Together they led Andrews to the Air Force's basketball championship.

That kept Tsioropoulos in shape for the Celtics, whom he joined in 1956. He spent two and a half seasons with Boston, where his career was derailed by a knee injury that required surgery early in his junior season at Kentucky. "Required" and "underwent" were two different things, though. Tsioropoulos played with torn cartilage that season, scoring 22 points in his only game before the injury, and averaging 7.5 in the games that followed.

"I had torn cartilage, but they didn't operate," he says. "Adolph got mad in '48 when they made him an assistant on the Olympic team. He wanted to be head coach, and in '52 he wanted [Kentucky] to win so he'd be head coach in the Olympics. I should not have played that season, but they sacrificed me. What did I know? But you can't single out coaches like Adolph or Bear Bryant. That was the era."

Tsioropoulos has paid a heavy price for being a part of that era. That left knee has been replaced, as was his left hip. He also has had two back surgeries doctors say stem from that 1951-52 season of knee pain.

"Too many surgeries," Tsioropoulos says.

Life worked out okay, though. Tsioropoulos spent his off seasons with the Celtics as a substitute teacher in Lynn, less than 15 miles away, earning enough to supplement his NBA salary while laying the foundation for his career to come. His first full-time teaching job was at Manual High School in Louisville in the spring of 1964, when he got married.

Jan Tsioropoulos became a successful mortgage banker, then president and CEO of a Louisville business, and Lou says she was the state's first female loan officer.

Together, they forged a comfortable life. Maybe the basketball side of things didn't entirely work out thanks to his educational ineligibility at Kentucky and balky knee with the Celtics, but Tsioropoulos knows things could have been a lot more difficult.

"I'm just glad I didn't have to go work in a tannery," he says. "That was too hard. Those people have more injuries than I had."

Where Have You Gone?

AMINU TIMBERLAKE

Life has moved on—and moved on quite nicely, thank you—for Aminu Timberlake since March 28, 1992.

As if you need to be reminded…that was the day of The Game: Duke's 104-103 victory over Kentucky in the NCAA Tournament's East Regional championship game. Some fans remember that day because of Duke forward Christian Laettner's shooting perfection—capped, in the final second, by The Shot. Others remember that day, and Laettner, for another reason: The Stomp.

Which brings us to Aminu Timberlake.

It was Timberlake's chest that received The Stomp, bringing a disproportionate measure of fame to a then-skinny Kentucky freshman who scored one point in that game, and averaged 1.1 points per game that season.

More than a decade later The Stomp has stuck with both parties, following Laettner around like a bad smell while lending a friendlier, most nostalgic tint to Timberlake's playing days. People tend to support an innocent victim, and on March 28, 1992, Timberlake was just that. Lying on the floor, underneath Laettner's shoe, Timberlake was helpless.

Today, he is not. Kentucky lost that day, and in the most basic sense Timberlake lost as well, but today he is a winner.

Well, no, that's not exactly right.

Today, Timberlake is a huge winner.

He's got a beautiful wife, Lisa; a beautiful daughter, Maya; a great job and a solid church family he mentions repeatedly in an interview for this book.

"All I can say is, hey, I've moved on," Timberlake says.

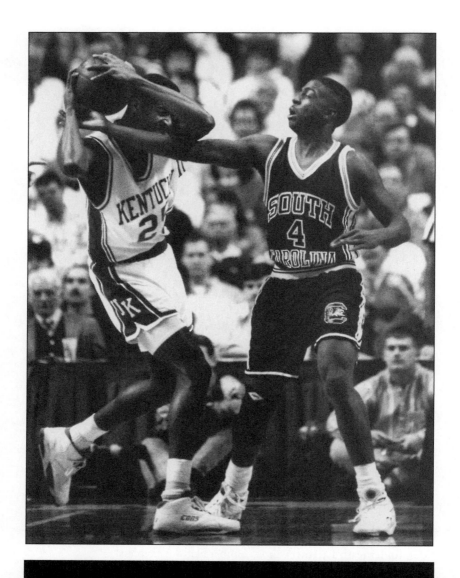

AMINU TIMBERLAKE

Years lettered: 1991-92, 1992-93
Career totals: 38 points, 47 rebounds

For Timberlake, his move began after the following season, when he transferred to Southern Illinois for his last two years of eligibility. No, he wasn't fleeing anything, certainly not The Stomp. After seeing his minutes dwindle to less than five per game as a sophomore, Timberlake left Kentucky in search of more playing time and a locale closer to his Chicago home. He found both on the campus in Carbondale, Illinois.

He also found his wife.

"Lisa, yes," Timberlake says, a smile coming over the phone. "Lisa was the best thing that happened to me at Southern Illinois."

Even as his life became a sailboat, Lisa became his anchor. After their graduation from Southern Illinois, she followed Aminu overseas as he pursued a professional playing career.

That's right—Aminu Timberlake made some money off the game of basketball. He was due, right? He made his money all over the world, in Korea and Hong Kong, New Zealand and Australia. Along the way Timberlake made something else, too. He made his playing weight.

Remember Timberlake as a Kentucky freshman, six foot nine and 195 pounds—so thin you wondered if Laettner's foot might snap him in half? It would be fun to see Laettner try that on the Timberlake who became a high-scoring forward overseas, a player who sailed past former Kentucky coach Rick Pitino's stated goal that he reach 230 pounds. By the time he finished his playing career, Timberlake was a sturdy 240 pounds.

"I finally reached Coach Pitino's weight," Timberlake says. "That was a goal."

Goals are big to Timberlake. They drove him to exceed on the court, and ultimately they drove him right out of basketball and right into corporate America. His choice, of course.

"I enjoyed my time in Korea, Hong Kong, Australia, you name it," Timberlake says. "It was a great opportunity for a city kid like myself to see the world. But it was time for me to make a decision on when and where I wanted to get started, and I remember talking to somebody who had played overseas. He said he had stopped playing basketball at 35, 38, something like that, and when he started interviewing [in the real world], people said to him, 'You have a nice basketball resume, but you've got to start [at the] entry level.'

"I was, what, 26? It was time for me, looking down the line, future-wise, to ask, 'Where do I want to be?' I wanted to start in corporate America as well as enjoy some form of stability and be a part of a church family, which was a great influence as I've been raising my daughter. I have no complaints."

No complaints, but plenty of goals still to be reached. Timberlake already has a nice home in Chicago, where nice homes don't come cheap. And he and Lisa are raising their daughter in a manner in which Aminu, as a youngster in a single-parent household, never had. But Timberlake, who plays pickup basketball around Chicago, still has much he wants to achieve off the court.

"You still need to set a goal and reach it," he says. "It's to your advantage if you are competitive. The game of basketball helps that a lot."

His first foray into corporate America was with a publishing company in Chicago, where he worked as an advertising consultant. Timberlake earned a degree in graphic design from Southern Illinois, but he says a friend from his church family was doing well in sales and told Timberlake he had the personality and the drive to be a winner in sales.

He has the drive, all right. Now working for the online job-placement giant CareerBuilder.com, Timberlake went into the 2004 year with a goal to be the No. 1 sales representative in a group that goes almost 40 strong, and at the end of the first quarter Timberlake was indeed ranked No. 1. That left three quarters to go, but Timberlake acted as if he could taste it already.

"I'm striving," he says. "I started here in December 2002 and now it's the No. 1 job board on the market, so I got in at a good time. It was a great chance to see this company take off."

And what of Aminu Timberlake? More than a decade later, has he finally ridded himself of the stigma of being at the wrong end of Christian Laettner's sneaker? Perhaps he finally has. In his time at CareerBuilder.com, he says, only once has a customer heard his name, done an audio double take, and asked if he was *that* Aminu Timberlake.

It's not like Timberlake will ever completely escape The Stomp, of course.

"It's brought up every year on ESPN Classic, but it's not a curse," he says. "To me, it didn't have anything to do with the outcome of the game, per se, but it adds to the drama, the legacy of that game. At the time it looked worse than what it was, but the referee caught him, justice was done, so on and so forth.

"That incident, it hasn't taken anything away from me. It was more of an honor to be associated with the University of Kentucky, and the details that were part of that game, but mainly going to the Final Four the next year and just being connected in some way or form to coach Pitino. Those are the things that have been to my advantage and may have opened up a few doors here or there. Kentucky basketball does take you a long way, even though I was there two years."

Life goes on, and sometimes it goes in the craziest of directions. With a name like Aminu Timberlake, he says his memorable moniker does evoke responses from customers, but usually they want to know one thing:

"Are you related to Justin Timberlake?"

Where Have You Gone?

BOB
BRANNUM

At Kentucky he became the youngest All-American in college basketball, but Bob Brannum wasn't good enough to finish his career at Kentucky. No, it doesn't make sense. But that's what happened.

He wasn't much of a golfer, but then Brannum became a golf pro and eventually a longtime, successful college golf coach. No, it doesn't make much sense. But that, too, is what happened.

In between Brannum, who passed away in early February of 2005, did a lot of different things. For example, he became known as one of the toughest guys in the NBA. And he sold candy door to door.

Of course it doesn't make sense. In a way, though, the nonsensical nature of Bob Brannum makes perfect sense, because he remained—after all these years—one of the more enigmatic characters in Kentucky basketball lore.

"You think people down there still remember me?" he wondered during our interview in late 2004.

A silly guy, that Bob Brannum. Sure, they remember.

When he arrived at Kentucky as a freshman in 1943, Brannum was a college basketball anomaly in many ways ... most notably because he arrived at Kentucky as a freshman in 1943. See, that was the middle of World War II, and most high school graduates were going straight from commencement to the U.S. armed forces, courtesy of the draft. Not Brannum. He graduated from high school in Winfield, Kansas, at age 16. He turned 17 that summer, but he was still too young for the draft, so he reported instead to Lexington, Kentucky, to serve under Adolph Rupp.

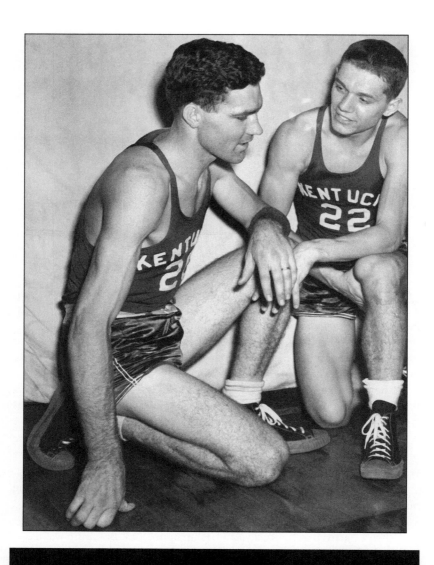

BOB BRANNUM
(LEFT)

Years lettered: 1943-44, 1946-47
Honors: All-SEC and All-American, 1943-44
Career totals: 379 points

That 1943-44 season saw Brannum become the star of the "Wildkittens," one of many nicknames given to a special team with few players older than 19. Rupp called them the "Beardless Wonders," and none was more wonderful than the six-foot-five Brannum, a center who averaged 12.1 points per game. That's not much of a scoring average by today's standards, but in 1944 it led the team by a wide margin and was Kentucky's highest individual scoring output in almost a decade.

Kentucky went 19-2, and Brannum was a consensus first-team All-American.

"Then I turned 18 that May," he said.

Eighteen was the magic number for the U.S. Army, which drafted Brannum a few months after the 1943-44 season ended and sent him to its Infantry Replacement Training Center at Fort Hood, Texas. Brannum must have been a model student, because he was chosen to attend cadre school and become an instructor himself.

In 1946, Brannum returned to Kentucky, but Kentucky had changed. These were no longer the Wildkittens or the Beardless Wonders, and he was no longer the most wonderful of them all. Through recruiting, Rupp had replaced what the military had taken away, and when Brannum returned he joined a team that no longer needed him to be a star.

Or even a starter.

Brannum averaged just 4.3 points in 1946-47, eighth on a team featuring Alex Groza, Ralph Beard and Wallace "Wah Wah" Jones. By the end of the season, Brannum wasn't even on the traveling roster. He was left at home for the prestigious (at the time) National Invitation Tournament, which Brannum took as a clear sign from Rupp that his services were no longer required, or even desired, at Kentucky.

"I had a baby girl and a wife, and Rupp was not happy with married people on his team," Brannum said. "My first year there [1943-44] I was married, but I was good enough he had to keep me. When I came back to Kentucky, he had a lot of players. He didn't play me a whole lot, and so I wasn't particularly happy there—and he wasn't happy with me."

Brannum had other options. While he had been in the army, a friend had tried to talk him into transferring to Michigan State instead of returning to Kentucky. After that 1946-47 season, Brannum called his friend and said he was ready to become a Spartan. He played one year with Michigan State, then was taken in another draft—by the Sheboygan Redskins of the NBA.

How good was Brannum? And how loaded was that Kentucky team of 1946-47? Look at it this way: Three years after averaging just 4.3 points for Kentucky, Brannum averaged 12.1 points as an NBA rookie in 1949-50.

His NBA career spanned five seasons spent with three franchises. Fort Wayne purchased him from Sheboygan and later traded him to the Boston Celtics. It was in Boston that Brannum made the contacts that would determine his post-basketball career, but first came his reputation as a tough guy, followed by his short-lived career in confections.

When Brannum was with Boston, word spread around the NBA that he was becoming something of a bodyguard for star Celtics point guard Bob Cousy. Players that roughed up the 5-11 Cousy would have to answer to the 6-5 Brannum, as legendary Syracuse Nationals center Dolph Schayes found out during one memorably bloody brawl.

"I was aggressive, and when I went to the pros I had to be aggressive," Brannum said. "They were all pretty tough. I didn't give crap to anybody, but I didn't take it, either."

Sounds like a formidable basketball player, but a lousy door-to-door candy salesman. And that's about what Brannum was as a salesman: lousy. So why'd he make the change? Money, if you can believe it. He says he quit the Celtics in 1955 at age 28 because he wasn't making enough to provide for a family that soon would grow to include six kids. Brannum got a job selling candy alongside the president of a local golf course, who made him an assistant golf pro despite the fact that, as a golfer, Brannum was typically good for about an 85. No matter. Brannum became an assistant golf pro, giving lessons for $2.50 an hour.

Meanwhile, Brannum was finishing up his bachelor's work by night at Boston University, earning the degree that would ultimately allow him to quit selling candy and become a coach.

"After I got my degree, Mr. [Walter] Brown, who owned the Celtics, called me and asked if I'd like to coach," Brannum said. "I'd never dreamed of coaching, but I wasn't a good salesman. So I said okay. He asked me to see a friend of his, Major General [Ernest N.] Harmon, who was president of Norwich University, a military school in Vermont. I was there seven years."

Brannum was a basketball coach and a golf coach at Norwich, positions he took seven years later at Kenyon College in Ohio before settling in at Brandeis for almost 30 years. Toward the end of his time at Brandeis, Brannum stopped coaching the basketball team—which won more than 200 games in his tenure, a school record—to focus on golf. By then Brannum had turned himself into one heck of a golfer, getting his handicap down to scratch with a personal-best round of 67.

Brannum's best golfer probably was Allen Doyle, the 2001 player of the year on the Senior PGA Tour. His best basketball player surely was John Rinka, a four-time All-American at Kenyon College who led Division III in scoring in 1970 at 41 points per game.

   Brannum never averaged half that many points in a season, but he still holds a record that went untouched by Rinka and everyone else to come along in the 60-plus years since Brannum starred for the Wildkittens. No one has ever become a consensus All-American at age 17, and with the best young players going straight from high school to the NBA, no one is likely to do it again.

Where Have You Gone?

JIM ANDREWS

Former Kentucky center Jim Andrews's story could have been a tragedy, or at least a travesty. His life could have headed irrevocably downhill after his aborted professional playing career in the mid-1970s, or after his divorce, or after his bankruptcy.

Could have.

Didn't.

Today Jim Andrews is happy and healthy, financially and otherwise, and he carries himself with a humility borne from brokenness.

"It hasn't always been easy," he says. "There was a time there where I said, 'Boy, am I off the right track.'"

That would be 1998, when a risky business venture backfired, leaving Andrews to file for bankruptcy in Lexington, Kentucky. It was about that same time that Andrews went to hear former Major League baseball player Doug Flynn, an outspoken Christian and a native of Lexington, give a talk to a local men's group.

"After hearing him speak, that's when I said, 'Boy, am I off track,'" Andrews says. "As I walked out of there that night, I realized everything I'd done, I'd done for selfish reasons. Once I got myself on track and doing the right things, things started falling into place."

Indeed, Andrews is back with the same company, Dubois Chemicals in Lexington, he left in the mid-1990s. He's happily remarried to a lady named Julie. He has even become close friends with Flynn, who jokes that Andrews's wife is the *real* Julie Andrews—even if she's not the famous one.

Being the famous Jim Andrews has come in handy at times, like when he plays in an annual celebrity golf tournament—the Children's Charity

JIM ANDREWS

Years lettered: 1970-71, 1971-72, 1972-73
Honors: All-SEC 1971-72, 1972-73
Career totals: 1,320 points (23rd in UK history), 783 rebounds
(12th in UK history), 153 assists

Classic—organized by Flynn, former Kentucky guard Kyle Macy and ex-Cincinnati Reds star Johnny Bench. Wildcats fans enjoy playing with the six-foot-11 Andrews, who finished his career 12th in the UK career scoring list (1,320 points) and seventh in rebounds (783). While he has slipped down both lists with the passage of time—and the return of freshman eligibility—Andrews entered the 21st century in the top 25 in both categories.

A fourth year of eligibility would have been nice for Andrews, but he was a man before his time for a lot of basketball reasons. For one thing, his years at Kentucky were strained by the awkward transition from Adolph Rupp to Joe B. Hall. Rupp's stars tended to be guards and forwards, not centers, while Hall built his teams around the likes of Andrews, Rick Robey, Sam Bowie and Melvin Turpin—big men pushing seven feet.

In his one season on the varsity for Rupp, Andrews was a reserve who averaged 6.5 points and five rebounds per game. In two seasons under Hall, after Rupp was forced out after reaching the state's mandatory retirement age, Andrews put up 20.8 points and 11.8 rebounds.

Timing? It's everything. That includes Andrews's professional basketball career. A big man with skill and a Kentucky pedigree, Andrews was drafted by both major U.S. professional leagues—but tried out for neither.

Andrews says he never got a chance to play for the Indiana Pacers, then with the ABA, because the Pacers' financial difficulties forced them to waive all their rookies from the 1973 draft. That still left Andrews with an opportunity in the NBA, with Seattle, but Andrews says a blunt phone call from Seattle coach Bill Russell scared him away.

"Bill Russell called and said, 'Look, I'm not going to have any white guys on my team. I'm just not,'" Andrews recalls. "When Seattle's management called, I told them what [Russell] had told me and they said, 'We want you to come out.' Thirty minutes later Bill Russell called again and said, 'I told you, don't bother.' I don't know if that was a game on his part. Some people have said he could do that to people. I took him at his word, and said this wasn't what I want to do. So I got drafted by Indiana and Seattle, and instead of two opportunities, I wound up with none."

Luckily for Andrews, there was a third opportunity: Europe. At the time, he says, the money overseas was comparable to what NBA rookies were making. It was a good deal, tax-free money for a shorter schedule of roughly 60 games. Andrews went to Italy and then Sweden, spending three years in Europe before returning home in 1976 at the behest of his first wife. He admits that quitting basketball was her idea, not his. He also admits that, in hindsight, he wasn't necessarily making the right decision.

"I was in a marriage where [my wife] was saying, 'When are you going to grow up, quit playing basketball, get a real job?'" Andrews says. "So I grew up, quit playing and got a real job."

That was with Dubois Chemicals, though he also spent several years in the late 1970s and early '80s as a graduate assistant coach on Hall's staff at Kentucky. With the Wildcats again, Andrews worked with big men—with his pupils including Mike Phillips, Robey, Bowie and Turpin.

Hall speaks highly of Andrews's coaching ability, saying he wishes Andrews would have remained on the bench. At the time, though, Andrews says he was making $258 a month as a part-time coach, with a monthly rent of $400.

"Coach Hall said eventually it would work out, but I went another direction," Andrews says. "Now, who knows? Hindsight may be 20-20. I may be one of those $3 million men [in college coaching], but it's too late for me to get back into the game."

Not necessarily. High school coaches in the Lexington area know Andrews is a willing tutor, and often they'll call for Andrews's help in developing a promising big man. Andrews says he enjoys that, as much for the instruction he gives to the high school coaches as to the big men themselves.

"It's a lot of fun," he says. "I'm trying to develop these guys as coaches as well, because they're only 25 or 30 or so, and they're eager to learn."

Andrews has learned plenty from his life's path. He shares what he can as an active member of the Fellowship of Christian Athletes, with a story that has a little something for anyone in his audience—from the highs of high school and college basketball stardom to the lows of divorce and bankruptcy to the highs of rejuvenation in all areas.

Remember that Children's Charity Classic, the fund-raising golf tournament that includes Andrews among its celebrity players? It's held at two Lexington-area golf courses, including the one where Andrews's home resides just off the ninth hole. Yes, life again has become good—very good—for Andrews, even after the devastation of divorce and bankruptcy. He and Julie have raised two children.

"Today we're very well off," Andrews says, not really talking about his bank account. "We've come out of this on the right track."

Where Have You Gone?

VERNON HATTON

In the early 1960s, before he cozied up to a microphone for the first time, Vernon Hatton was already famous in Lexington. The question is—what was he famous for? If you were a Kentucky fan, you had your choice:

Hatton's 47-footer at the end of overtime against Temple in December 1957? His running, twisting lay-up in the final seconds to win the Wildcats' 1958 national semifinal, also against Temple? His epic scoring duel with Seattle University's Elgin Baylor in the 1958 NCAA championship game?

Hatton has a good idea which memory looms largest in the minds of Kentucky Nation, and it's neither of his outstanding performances from the 1958 Final Four. He believes he has become synonymous with that half-court heave at the first overtime buzzer against Temple, forcing a second overtime—and eventually leading to a third, where Hatton put an end to one of the longest games in Kentucky history with six points to cap the Wildcats' 85-83 victory at Memorial Coliseum.

"Everywhere I go, people always say they were there," Hatton says. "I know there's been at least 15 to 20,000 people who have told me that—and Memorial Coliseum only holds about 11,000."

Sounds like more than a few people have been telling some tall tales—just the way Hatton likes it. After his playing career was finished, including four years in the NBA with the Philadelphia Warriors and St. Louis Hawks, Hatton became a Lexington auctioneer. He got paid to stretch the truth ever so slightly, and that's by his own admission.

"Auctioneers have a license to exaggerate a little bit," Hatton says. "That's what an auction is—it's a fable. Part truth, part fiction."

VERNON HATTON

Years lettered: 1955-56, 1956-67, 1957-58
Honors: All-SEC and All-American, 1957-58; retired jersey No. 52
Career totals: 1,153 points (37th in UK history), 346 rebounds

The truth is, for almost 40 years Hatton was one of the best auctioneers in the state because of his unbeatable combination of name recognition, playful personality and locomotive mouth. The name recognition got Hatton gigs. His personality got people to sit down and stay a while. And his mouth had them digging into their pockets for money.

During an interview for this book, Hatton put those final two qualities on display when he seized a brief moment of silence to ask, "Do you want me to chant for you?"

And off he went. What came out of his mouth next sounded something like this:

"Hmmmmmmm-mmmmmm-twenty now-hmmmmmm-twenty-five-hmmm-rmmmm-bmmmm-SOLD ... to the man picking his nose!"

Hatton paused, then said calmly, "Everyone picks their nose, you know."

He's a natural, Vernon Hatton, probably as capable an auctioneer as he was a basketball player—and he was a pretty darned capable basketball player. He was a big guard in the late 1950s, standing almost six foot four and weighing 195 pounds, and he used that size to average 15.2 points and 4.6 rebounds in 76 career games at Kentucky. He was an All-American as a senior, when he led the "Fiddlin' Five" to the 1958 national championship and cemented his reputation as perhaps the most clutch 'Cat ever. First there was that 47-footer against Temple in the regular season, then his driving basket with 16 seconds left against those same Owls to win the national semifinal, 61-60. Then, there was his 30-point explosion against Seattle in the Wildcats' 84-72 championship victory. Baylor led Seattle with 25 points, though he needed 32 field-goal attempts—12 more than Hatton—to get his points.

Baylor, though, was named Most Outstanding Player of that Final Four.

"I'm still mad to this day about that," says Hatton, who believes that he or teammate Johnny Cox (24 points, 16 rebounds in the title game) would have been a better choice. "Baylor was a big All-American for two or three years, but we won. It still makes me mad when I talk about it. Oh, well—we got the big trophy."

They also got the cool nickname, the "Fiddlin' Five," a moniker that came straight from the top: Coach Adolph Rupp, in the preseason, noting that his team didn't have the star power necessary to make a run at a national title: "We're fiddlers, that's all," he said. "They're pretty good fiddlers—be right entertaining at a barn dance. But I'll tell you, you need violinists to play at Carnegie Hall. We don't have any violinists."

No, but Hatton went on to make music—and some decent money—with his mouth after his NBA career ended on a one-two punch of his own making. The first blow was his decision to leave the Hawks in 1962 to witness the birth of Terry, his second of three sons. The Hawks basically told him not to bother coming back to St. Louis, but several weeks later the team changed its tune when center Clyde Lovellette got hurt and management asked Hatton to fill the big man's roster spot. Hatton declined, and to this day he wonders if that was the right thing to do.

"As the years go by, I'm sorry I didn't go when they called me back to St. Louis," Hatton says. "There were only eight teams in the league in those days, so a place on the NBA roster was pretty special."

Regrets? Apparently Hatton has a few, though his auctioneering career seems to have given him as much satisfaction as his basketball career. Hatton will tell you he's the world's biggest auctioneer in one instant, then confirm it by telling you he's six-foot-four, 300 pounds. Then he'll make a play on the word 'colonel,' which is the affectionate title given to auctioneers.

"Auctioneers are called 'colonels,' and the definition of a kernel is the inside of a nut," Hatton says. "So that's what I am."

His little acorns didn't fall far from the tree. All three of Hatton's boys (Jeff, Terry and Steve) also are auctioneers, which means they can probably all tell a story. An auctioneer's world is one of tall tales—the taller, the better—and Hatton loves telling stories about himself to loosen up his audience. One of his favorites is the time Rupp shouted at him for constantly losing his composure.

"I was in awe of him, and I could barely talk. Every time I got around Coach Rupp I'd stutter, I'd be so scared: 'C-c-c-coach,'" Hatton says, nearing his favorite part of the story—the punch line. "He'd say, 'My God, Hatton, I don't know how you're going to get through school. You'll have to be a coach, preacher or auctioneer.' I became an auctioneer, and now my stuttering is good as I call bids."

Hatton even cracks on his trademark college play, that 47-footer against Temple in the final second of overtime—suggesting that maybe, just maybe, he had more than the alleged one second to get off the shot.

"It was a two-hand set shot, and I threw it in from the side," he says. "I was all lined up, with my hands ready, so all I had to do was throw it. But, you know, we were at home, and one second at home makes it about five seconds. So I had plenty of time to make a one-second shot."

Ask Hatton if it's true—the Rupp story, the 47-footer story, any story—and he's ready.

"That's what you'll have to figure out," he says.

MELVIN TURPIN

Two or three more hours, and Melvin Turpin would have died.

That's what doctors told him in 2003, when he visited a walk-in clinic complaining of chronic thirst and fatigue. Doctors took a blood sample but didn't have to bother with a microscope. One look, and they knew something was terribly wrong.

"My blood was almost black," Turpin says. "I had no water in my body."

Turpin, one-half of Kentucky's Twin Towers with Sam Bowie in the early 1980s, was rushed to a hospital where he spent nearly two weeks. The diagnosis: Type I Diabetes, a manageable disease with proper care but fatal if untreated. Turpin didn't know he had become diabetic until doctors told him.

"They said I was very, very lucky," Turpin says. "Another couple hours walking around thirsty and tired and I probably wouldn't have lived."

That kind of close call will make for one happy former basketball player, and that's exactly what Turpin is today. A mid-day phone call for this book awoke Turpin, who often works the night shift as a security guard, but he quickly went from groggy to giddy as he described his most unusual life.

Life after Kentucky has been unusual for Turpin for a number of reasons, including the obligatory basketball references, but it has been most unusual—and most pleasing—because he married one of his former high school teachers.

Nearly seven years after he had played the last of his 361 games in the NBA, Turpin was back home in Lexington when he bumped into his former health teacher, Kerry Soper. This was 1997, nearly two decades after he had graduated from Lexington's Bryan Station High School, and Turpin asked Soper if she remembered him. Of course, Soper told the nearly seven-footer.

MELVIN TURPIN

Years lettered: 1980-81, 1982-83, 1983-84, 1984-85
Honors: All-SEC and All-American, 1983-84; All-SEC 1982-83
Career totals: 1,509 points (13th in UK history), 730 rebounds, 76 assists, 226 blocks (2nd in UK history)

He asked Soper if she would go out with him. Of course, Soper said.

In 2004, Melvin and Kerry Turpin celebrated their sixth wedding anniversary.

"I had a huge crush on her in high school," Turpin says. "All these years later, I came to find out I still did."

Turpin had done some fascinating things since he and Soper had met at Bryan Station High in the late 1970s. First, he played at Kentucky, where he finished his career in 1984 among the school's top ten in career points and rebounds. Then he played in the NBA, going No. 6 overall in the 1984 draft after this amazing run of players was drafted first through fifth: Hakeem Olajuwon, Sam Bowie, Michael Jordan, Sam Perkins, Charles Barkley. With the sixth pick Turpin was taken ten spots ahead of another future superstar, John Stockton.

Turpin's career wasn't anywhere near as long or fruitful as that of Jordan, Barkley, Stockton or Olajuwon, but it had its moments. In his second year in the league, Turpin averaged 13.7 points and seven rebounds for Cleveland in 1986. He never approached those numbers again and retired from the NBA in 1990 after five seasons (he had played the 1988-89 season overseas).

"I kind of got tired of it," he says. "My knees had been bothering me really bad, and I got tired. I finally said, 'That's it, I'm done.'"

Weight was an issue. Turpin arrived at Kentucky at a svelte 6-11, 240 pounds, but early into his NBA career he started to push 300 pounds. Turpin's contracts began to include weight clauses, and he was dubbed "Dinner Bell." The weight took its toll on his knees, but the hassle of being considered overweight took its toll on his heart.

"I got tired of dealing with it," he says. "Back then the NBA wanted its big men to be thin, but now everyone has a player who weighs 285, 300 pounds. They don't care any more."

Turpin had made so much money from professional basketball that he didn't have to work after he retired from the NBA—so he didn't. He lived a few years in Illinois, then returned to Lexington. He says he watched so much daytime television that he became a "soap [opera] addict," and when he left the house it was to hunt or fish. Sometimes he'd join his former Kentucky coach, Joe B. Hall, for some fishing on Hall's land in nearby Cynthiana. Sometimes Turpin would go fishing at Hall's place with a group of ex-players: Bowie, Kenny Walker, Jim Master, and Dicky Beal.

"Coach didn't even have to be there," Turpin says. "We'd get fishing poles out of his garage and go."

Turpin and Soper were married in 1998, and it was his new bride who prodded him to get out of his television-and-fishing rut and back into the work force. Turpin, whose weight had climbed to well over 300 pounds, says he put up a fuss at first.

"I'm still making some money [from basketball], and my retirement kicks in soon. I ain't broke," he says, booming a big laugh. "I sat on my butt for a good ten years and I was okay, but pretty soon you've got to find something else to do. It just got boring, and pretty soon my wife said, 'You can find a job, or you can start doing housework.' I found a job."

Turpin booms another big laugh, but his first job was no laughing matter. He became a teacher's aide at an alternative school in Lexington, where the student body was composed of kids who had been kicked out of other high schools for disciplinary reasons.

"I only spent a year there, and it was time to go," Turpin says. "We always had fights, kids getting arrested. Those kids were cussing all the time. I had to find something else."

Turpin took a job as a security officer, a position where his size has been a help and a hindrance. It helps to be nearly seven feet tall and close to 300 pounds when asking someone rowdy to please settle down. It hurts, though, when people constantly recognize the former Kentucky basketball star and ask for autographs when he's on the job. That's why Turpin says he turns down assignments to work security for Kentucky's home games at Rupp Arena.

"I'm big, and everybody recognizes me," he says. "If I went to Rupp, I wouldn't be able to do my job."

Doing his job sometimes means handling scary situations. Turpin has been assigned for more than a year to a Nissan dealership in Lexington, where he often draws the night shift. That means patrolling the perimeter of the lot, including going behind the main building where it can get awfully dark after midnight. In certain situations, Turpin wonders if his size might even work against him.

"You might find three or four people around back at four in the morning," he says. "I see the fear in people's eyes, but these days you have to be very careful. These kids don't mess around. These kids carry knives or guns, so you've got to watch out for yourself and them. You try to be as nice as you can, but you don't know what might come up."

Turpin keeps a gun in his car, just to be safe, but he's more cautious than scared. He has faced death once before, that 2003 scare with diabetes, and he survived. He has to take daily insulin shots to regulate his blood-sugar level, but it's a discomfort he can handle.

There are worse alternatives.

"I'm on the needle, but I'm alive," he says. "Everything is fine with me."

Where Have You Gone?

WALLACE "WAH WAH" JONES

More than a half-century after his victorious college finale in the 1949 NCAA championship game, Wallace "Wah Wah" Jones remains the most impressive athlete ever churned out by the University of Kentucky. He was an All-SEC performer in three sports and the owner of a retired school jersey in basketball and football. So here's something that shouldn't surprise a soul:

Old No. 27's mojo didn't end with graduation.

Since his days as a Wildcat, almost everything else Jones touched has been a success—including two lawsuits, four business ventures and his run at sheriff as a Republican in a strong Democratic county.

"Life has been good to me," Jones says.

Better than good. Try fabulous.

Jones is a native of Harlan, Kentucky, where he made varsity in eighth grade and scored a then-national record 2,398 points in his high school career. But, he's better-known as a member of one of the most famous basketball teams in Kentucky history, the 1947-48 group that won the program's first of seven NCAA championships. That team's starting lineup (Jones, Ralph Beard, Alex Groza, Cliff Barker and Kenny Rollins) became known as the Fabulous Five. The quintet helped the Wildcats go 36-3, swept five spots on the All-SEC team and went en masse to the 1948 Olympics at London, where they led the United States to the gold medal.

Jones played nearly every minute of the Wildcats' 58-42 victory against Baylor in the NCAA title game at Madison Square Garden. It was no big deal for someone who also was a two-way end on Bear Bryant's Kentucky

Photo courtesy of Wallace Jones

WALLACE "WAH WAH" JONES

Years lettered: 1945-46, 1946-47, 1947-48, 1948-49
Honors: All-SEC and All-American, 1948-49; All-SEC 1945-46,
1946-47, 1947-48; retired jersey No. 27
Career totals: 1,151 points (38th in UK history)

football team and a two-way player (pitcher, outfielder) for the Kentucky baseball team. Jones also ran track—no, not the decathlon.

The lazy bum.

Just kidding. Jones's productivity in college was a foreshadowing of what was to come after his athletic career. First, though, came three seasons with the Indianapolis Olympians of the NBA, where Jones was a career 10.2-point scorer and joined three other Fabulous Five teammates (Groza, Beard and Barker) to help spark the merger between two warring leagues. Spurred in part by the popularity of the Fabulous Five, the National Basketball League and Basketball Association of America united to form what is known to this day as the NBA.

"We owned the Indianapolis team," Jones says, not exaggerating. "The [NBL] told us they'd give us the franchise if we'd come as a unit, with Beard and Groza and Barker. We picked up Joe Holland, and the two leagues were battling, and the prices were going up, and when [the BAA] saw us going in the other league, they negotiated the leagues getting together. So we were instrumental in the two leagues getting together."

Ownership didn't last long. The NBA took the franchise from the Kentucky players in 1954 after the point-shaving scandal that ended the careers of Beard and Groza. Because of his Kentucky connection, Jones was routinely—and mistakenly—lumped into the point-shaving scandal along with Beard and Groza, though he was never found guilty. Jones took on two magazines that continued to make that mistake in print, and he says he won a pair of libel lawsuits.

"They got used to printing 'Beard, Groza and Jones,' and it went that way for a while," Jones says. "I was never even questioned. So I won two different lawsuits."

That was seed money for Jones's first entrepreneurial venture five years later, but first came perhaps the most improbable victory of his entire life— the elected post of Fayette County sheriff. Dating back to the Civil War, Fayette County has been a Democratic stronghold. That includes the year 2005, and it certainly included the year 1953. Well sir, the local Republican party was absolutely tired of losing to the Democrats, so when Wallace "Wah Wah" Jones returned to Fayette County, they asked the famous Fabulous Five star if he would run for sheriff. Jones had never thought about politics or law enforcement, but his basketball career had ended after a knee injury during the 1952 season, and he was looking for something to do. Sheriff? Why not?

Jones had more than his Kentucky pedigree going for him. He also had a nickname that remains, to this day, among the most memorable in Big Blue history. The nickname was a creation of his younger sister, who as a baby couldn't spit out her brother's given name and settled for "Wah Wah." Everyone else just kind of followed along. After a while, Jones says, the only people who called him Wallace were his wife and Bear Bryant.

"The nickname stuck in a lot of people's minds," Jones says. "People around here, following UK the way they do, they knew it. And I had all the little kids wearing Indian hats that said, 'Wah Wah for Sheriff.'"

Jones won that election, serving as sheriff from 1954-58. In those days, he says, Fayette County term limits wouldn't allow him to run for the same office again, so Jones ran for Congress in 1958 and lost. Still, politics paid off in two ways. First, while running for Congress he visited the White House and had his picture taken with President Eisenhower. Second, while serving as sheriff he had taken note of a struggling, one-van company that offered tours of the Lexington horse-farm industry. Jones thought he saw some promise in the venture, so in 1959 he used the money from his libel lawsuits to purchase Bluegrass Tours.

One old van became a fleet of new vans, then a Greyhound bus, then a fleet of buses. Today, Bluegrass Tours houses its 17 buses in a $1 million facility with two full-time mechanics among more than 10 employees. After getting that company up and running, Jones turned the business over to Wallace Jr.—he and Edna's only son among three children—and looked for another business opportunity.

He found it on a neighbor's roof.

"We didn't have any TV stations in (Lexington) at that time," Jones says. "We had to use the antennae on our roofs to get three channels in Cincinnati, two in Louisville and maybe one in Huntington, West Virginia, but we didn't have any source of programming information. The newspaper would put out one line, but no detail."

Jones changed that, creating a magazine he called *TV in the Bluegrass*. The biggest hurdle to the magazine's success was creating a healthy number of subscribers, a hurdle he cleared like a street curb thanks to his ingenuity and name recognition. The ingenuity: He went to every house in the area with an antennae and stuck a flyer in the front door advertising his magazine. The name recognition: He went to the local U.S. Post Office to get a P.O. box for his subscribers to use, and was recognized by a postal clerk who said he had just the box number available—No. 27.

That was Jones's number at Kentucky, of course.

"I wanted a number people could remember," Jones says. "I figure they remembered No. 27 pretty easily."

After eight or nine years, *TV Guide* came into the marketplace and Jones sold his subscriber list. Then he started another magazine, this one aimed at Lexington's growing entertainment industry. He called it *Around the Town*

Lexington and printed information about hotels and restaurants in town. The trick was selling advertising, but for Wah Wah Jones, that was a pretty easy trick.

"My advertisers, I just walk in town and sign them up," says Jones, who ran that magazine from 1970 to 1998. "Everyone from town knows me, and I know all the owners and different people. When I go in and see them, it's no problem at all."

Life has been no problem at all for one of Kentucky's most famous athletes. He even turned *Leonard's Losers* into a winner, running a Lexington-based franchise of the well-known Southern football prognostication magazine until 2004, when he retired.

Along the way, Jones picked up a matching set of clocks given by the SEC to players the league has recognized as "legends" in football or basketball. Jones is the only one to earn such recognition in both sports, getting the football award at the 1996 SEC championship game in Atlanta, and the basketball award at the 2001 SEC tournament in Nashville. Both clocks are in his son's office at Bluegrass Tours.

As he looks back on his life, Jones mulls only one "what if?" What if he had gone to that tryout in the late 1940s with the Boston Braves, the Major League Baseball team that wanted to give him a look at pitcher? This was college football season, and Jones remembers approaching his coach, Bear Bryant, for permission.

"He looked at me real hard and said, 'Are you going to play football or are you going to play baseball?'" Jones says. "I decided to play football."

A legend was born.

Where Have You Gone?

TRAVIS FORD

After graduating from Kentucky as perhaps the greatest shooter in school history, Travis Ford knew he had several career options—but acting wasn't supposed to be one of them. Acting? Other than the occasional flop during a basketball game, Ford had never acted in his life.

Ford was a basketball guy, and if he wasn't going to stay involved in the game as a player or coach, he was going to be a financial guy. He had already passed his stockbroker's exam, and he believed he could use his academic acumen—he was a three-time academic All-SEC pick—on Wall Street.

But then the phone rang ...

It was early 1995. Ford had recently returned to Kentucky from the West Coast after getting cut by the Golden State Warriors. Unsure what to do next, he took the stockbroker's exam and passed it. Ford spent the next week trying to figure out his next move when the phone rang. It was an executive from Touchstone Pictures in California, and the guy was saying the most unlikely thing. The movie exec was saying he was working on a movie that had a part that was perfect for Ford.

"It was incredible," Ford says. "I'd never wanted to act. I'd never even thought about acting. Never."

Still, Ford listened. What could it hurt? He listened as the Touchstone executive talked about the movie, describing *The Sixth Man* as a basketball picture about a college program whose best player dies before the NCAA Tournament and returns as a ghost to help his old team. Ford's role? Danny O'Grady, a hotheaded but gifted player who had to be portrayed by someone who could really play the game. Not many Hollywood actors could play

49

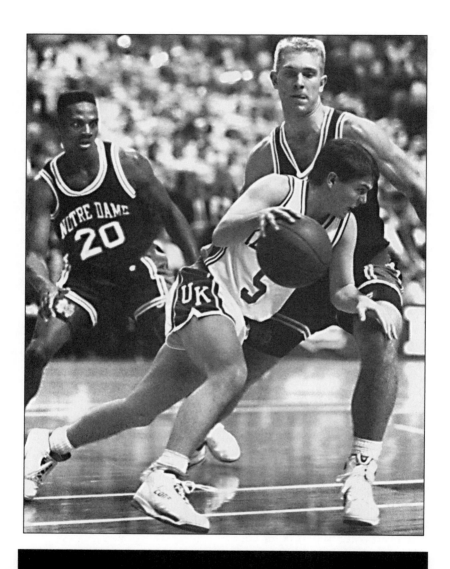

TRAVIS FORD

Years lettered: 1991-92, 1992-93, 1993-94
Honors: All-SEC 1992-93
Career totals: 951 points, 201 rebounds, 428 assists (8th in UK history), 190 three-pointers (3rd in UK history)

at the level Touchstone wanted, and so movie executives had spent the previous year watching college games, looking for the right guy.

And they spotted Ford—Kentucky's scrappy little point guard who had picture-perfect shooting form, a friendly face and a fiery attitude.

O'Grady's character wasn't going to get star billing, but it was what Hollywood people called a "principle role." An actor in a principle role gets paid handsomely, and if Ford was going to do it, he'd have to move to the West Coast for several months, maybe longer, until the shooting was finished.

As the conversation unfolded, Ford couldn't believe what he was hearing. As the conversation ended, Ford couldn't believe what he was saying. He was saying yes.

"They flew me out to California, to Los Angeles, for a screen test," he says. "The director wanted me for the part, but the executive producers didn't know who I was, so the director and a couple other people put me with an acting coach before the audition to be prepared. They put me with the coach for two or three days, then auditioned me in front of the producers and everyone else. Three or four days later they called and offered me the role."

The movie, alas, wasn't embraced by critics. The stars were big enough— Marlon Wayans and Kadeem Hardison—but the idea was a bit sappy, okay? A ghost coming back to help his former team in the NCAA Tournament?

Still, Ford says he got a lot out of a process that took nearly 18 months from start to finish. First, while he won't say how much he was paid, he will say, "It was good—it was well worth it." Second, he says he made several lasting friendships while on the set, including some with actors who had spent almost 15 years in the business without landing the kind of plum part that fell into Ford's lap.

"They gave me grief every single day," he says.

And finally, Ford's time in the movie business drove home the point that he was meant for a career not in Hollywood or on Wall Street, but in basketball.

"It was a great experience," he says. "It gave me a little time to get away from basketball, actually, and re-energized me. It made me realize how much I loved the game, and how much I wanted to coach."

Fine, but where? Ford didn't know, but he knew he'd have options. His most likely avenue was to join the staff of a small Division I program somewhere—anywhere—and work his way up the ladder. To prepare, Ford returned home to Kentucky and attended Wildcats practices, soaking up Rick Pitino's knowledge from the perspective of a budding coach.

And then the phone rang.

By now it was the spring of 1997. Ford was by no means old or even getting old—he was only 27—but he was older than most former players trying to get into the coaching business. For one thing, his college career had taken five years thanks to his transfer from Missouri, which meant spending a year on the sidelines as a redshirt before becoming eligible for Kentucky's 1991-92 season. For another, he had spent 18 months with the movie, then another few months waiting for the 1996-97 season to finish and coaching opportunities to arise.

The opportunity that came wasn't what he had been expecting. It was better.

A family friend was an alumnus of Campbellsville University, an NAIA school in central Kentucky. Campbellsville needed a new coach, and the family friend put Ford in touch with the school's president, Ken Winters.

"Dr. Winters knew me from playing for Kentucky, and he liked my background in academics," Ford says. "He saw me as a player who understood the game and succeeded because of my knowledge of the game, not necessarily my abilities."

And that's how Travis Ford, who had never coached a day in his life, woke up one morning in 1997 as the head coach of Campbellsville University. In some ways it was similar to his movie experience, going into a major role with no experience. In some ways, it was harder—much harder.

"The three years I spent there were the hardest-working years I'd put in to that point," Ford says. "When you become a coach, you thought you'd worked hard as a player. You thought you'd put in a lot of time. But it's nothing compared to the time you have to put in as a coach. At Campbellsville I was young, a single guy at the time, and I just about spent 24 hours a day in the office. At that level you coach, fundraise—you do everything. I grew up quick."

He won quick, too.

In three seasons his teams went 67-31, including a 28-3 year that saw him earn Mid-South Conference coach of the year honors. When the head coaching position opened in March 2000 at Division I Eastern Kentucky, Ford was an obvious choice. Being a former Wildcat would help him win over fans and recruits, and his three seasons at Campbellsville demonstrated his ability to win on the court as well.

At Eastern Kentucky, Ford inherited a mess. The Richmond, Kentucky, campus might only have been 30 miles southeast of Lexington, but the basketball program was light years from what Ford had seen at Rupp Arena. The EKU team hadn't had a winning season in almost a decade. Fan support was minimal.

"It had really fallen off the map," Ford says. "It wasn't like rebuilding a program—it was almost like starting one. Eastern Kentucky had gotten itself in a rut and just hadn't gotten itself out, for whatever reason. But I saw a lot of opportunity here: very good facilities, beautiful campus, big university, and they wanted to make a commitment to basketball. I saw it was going to take time, but I liked the potential."

Ford's first team returned just two lettermen from a 6-21 bunch, and while the results on the court weren't all that tangible—Eastern Kentucky went 7-19—fans liked Ford's pedigree and his up-tempo offense. Attendance increased 91 percent from the previous season.

The Colonels improved to 14-15 by 2003-04, their best record in a dozen years, and finished a respectable 8-8 in the Ohio Valley Conference. Ford followed that with his best recruiting class.

In 2004-05, Eastern Kentucky won a program-best 22 games and reached the NCAA Tournament, where the Colonels faced—of all teams—Kentucky in the opening round.

"You can't tell me that was an accident," Ford says.

Ford nearly knocked off his alma mater, throwing a 72-64 scare into the heavily favored Wildcats before a crowd of nearly 30,000 in Indianapolis. The crowd seemed to be torn between their current Kentucky heroes and their former one.

Eastern Kentucky might have finished off the Wildcats if a couple of Ford's players could shoot as well as their coach once did. Fat chance, though. Ford's 52.9-percent accuracy from three-point range as a junior in 1992-93 remains a Kentucky season record. He ranks second in Kentucky history at 88.2 percent on his career on free throws, and his 15 assists in a December 1993 game remains the program's top one-game total.

The opponent in that 1993 game? Eastern Kentucky.

"I didn't tell my players about that," Ford says. "I don't think they'd care."

Ford has new players to coach now. He parlayed that breakthrough season at Eastern Kentucky into the coaching position at Massachusetts, whose fans have the same passion for basketball as their new head coach. The 2005-06 season will be his first in Amherst, Mass.

"People here, they love their basketball," Ford says. "I'm going to be very happy at UMass."

Ford has no plans to tell his new players about *The Sixth Man*, which earned a spot on the movie-review web site *Rotten Tomatoes*.

Let the critics think what they want. Ford has three huge fans of his role as Danny O'Grady, his children: Brooks, Kyleigh and Shane.

"They like to watch it," Ford says. "Go figure."

Where Have You Gone?

DWANE CASEY

To Dwane Casey, they were small acts of kindness. Nothing more or less. How could he know that he was planting seeds that would bloom, years later, to rescue him when his world came crashing down?

The Japanese man's name was Motoka Kohoma. He spent much of the 1979-80 college basketball season in Lexington, Kentucky, soaking up whatever knowledge he could get from Wildcats coach Joe B. Hall. Kohoma came to practices and games, studied film, even lived for a time in a vacant room in the players' dormitory. He was determined to become a better basketball coach, but he was a lonely figure.

Casey's heart went out to the Japanese man. Nothing more, nothing less. Anyone who knew Dwane Casey at the time wouldn't have been surprised, because Casey never got sucked into the notion that, as a member of the big-time college basketball establishment, he was a big-time person in his own right.

During his four seasons as a reserve guard from 1975-79, Casey became known around the Kentucky athletic department as a go-to guy. Need a player to speak against drugs at a local elementary school? Go to Casey. Need a player to deliver a graduation speech at a high school in Hazard? Go to Casey. Need a player to visit a basketball fan in a Frankfort hospital? Go to Casey.

"I felt like I was an ambassador during my years at Kentucky," Casey says. "I took the responsibility of being a Kentucky player very seriously. I drove my little Toyota Celica lift-back all over the state."

During that 1979-80 season, which Casey spent on the coaching staff as a graduate assistant, he gravitated toward Kohoma. At practices he demon-

DWANE CASEY

Years lettered: 1975-76, 1976-77, 1977-78, 1978-79
Career totals: 125 points, 51 rebounds, 62 assists
Assistant coach: 1987-89

strated techniques and tried to explain their terminology, and eventually he began giving Kohoma rides to and from practice. They went out to dinner together, even hung out in the sauna at the old Wildcat Lodge.

"I felt sorry for him," Casey says. "Here's a guy who was around all the time, didn't speak any English. I just reached out to him. They were just small acts of kindness."

Eight years later, Casey was a rising star in college coaching. He had spent five years on Clem Haskins's staff at Western Kentucky, and in 1986 he returned to his alma mater to join Eddie Sutton's staff. On an April weekend in 1988, he was invited to interview for the head coaching vacancy at the University of New Orleans.

That weekend—that very weekend—Casey's world collapsed.

In Los Angeles, a young employee of Emery Worldwide Air Freight claimed to have found an open envelope with $1,000 cash. The envelope was addressed from Casey to Claude Mills, the father of Los Angeles high school basketball star Chris Mills. The employee leaked the alleged contents of the envelope to the local newspaper, and soon Kentucky was in the middle of an NCAA investigation.

There were other elements to that NCAA investigation—most notably Eric Manuel's ACT score—but the Casey-Mills connection was always mentioned prominently. Sutton and Casey have always maintained that Kentucky never sent Mills money. Mills's father says he never received money. Mills's high school coach, Harvey Kitani, says the envelope had no money, and it was Kitani who first opened it.

"The only person who says there was money in it was this kid from Emery," Casey says.

And what of that kid? Subsequent media reports would call him a UCLA basketball fan. The late 1980s was a difficult time to be a UCLA fan, with John Wooden's dynasty already crumbled and the best recruits from southern California leaving for schools like Michigan, LSU and Kentucky. Given all that, is it that much of a stretch to believe a UCLA fan would do something drastic to stem the tide of Los Angeles players heading East? Something drastic like concoct a story about an opened envelope, and $1,000 in cash?

It's possible. Anything is possible. The reality is this: The entire Kentucky staff would resign after the 1988-89 season, and the NCAA would place Kentucky on three years of probation and Casey on five years of probation.

That April 1988 job interview with New Orleans? Casey still went, but on the heels of the worst weekend of his life, he knew he had no chance. The job went to Tim Floyd, who later moved on to Iowa State and then to the NBA.

When he was interviewed for this book in late 2004, Casey was the associate head coach of the Seattle SuperSonics, a promising NBA assistant who had been approached by four different franchises about becoming their head coach. It hadn't happened yet, but Casey remained hopeful. In the meantime, Casey and Floyd had crossed paths all the time, and Floyd still joked with him: "Thanks for not getting that job at New Orleans."

Casey laughs, and the reason he can laugh is Motoka Kohoma. Nearly a decade after his visit to the University of Kentucky, Kohoma still remembered Casey, and in 1990 he called Casey to offer a job.

"I was sitting at home when he called me," Casey says. "Over there it was day time, but it was late at night in Lexington. I was sitting there, not knowing which way I was going to go, when he called me and said he was starting a new [professional] team in Japan. He called out of nowhere. That was the last place I was expecting to resume coaching. I thought I'd be doing something else for a few years in the United States before getting back into it."

Casey accepted and spent the next five years coaching in Japan. He still dreamed of coaching in the United States, though by the early 1990s he had set his sights on the NBA. To reach that goal he returned in the summers to coach in the NBA summer league in Los Angeles, but by early 1994 he hadn't been offered a full-time coaching job in his home country.

"I thought I was never going to get back," Casey says. "A lot of nights [in Japan] I said, 'Whoa, I'm a long way from anywhere, and nobody in America cares who wins this game or loses this game. Nobody cares who didn't block out or execute.' I had a lot of times like that, but in hindsight it was a blessing for me. I found out about myself that I didn't need the adulation and pats on the back and bright lights to do something I really loved. It made me appreciate the craft of coaching.

"I did a lot of reading, soul searching. It was a blessing in disguise. I wouldn't want to go through that lesson again, but it helped me become a better coach, a better teacher."

Then it happened. Before the 1994-95 NBA season, Sonics coach George Karl offered Casey a job on his staff.

The Sonics had brought Casey back into the game, but he knew whom else to thank: Motoka Kohoma.

"I go to Japan every summer to do clinics, and every time I go back, no matter where I am, I look [Kohoma] up and try to see him," Casey says. "At that age, in college, you really take your friendships for granted. I was just reaching out to someone who seemed like he needed a friend. You see a guy there by himself. ... It's just amazing that so many years later the friendship would come full circle, and he helped me get my feet on the ground in coaching. I'd have never thought, all those years down the road, this same guy would turn around and be able to help me."

A loyal guy, Casey had stayed with the Sonics for a decade, an unheard-of tenure for an assistant coach—especially considering the Sonics have been through three head coaches along the way. Karl was replaced in 1998 by Paul Westphal, who was replaced in 2000 by Nate McMillan. Over the years Casey says he'd had "countless" opportunities to join other staffs in the NBA, but he had only considered leaving the Sonics for a head coaching job.

By 2000, Casey was among the most marketable assistants in the NBA. Since then, the Bucks, Pistons, Hawks and Raptors (twice) have interviewed him for their vacancies, though each time the job went to someone who had either been a head coach in college or had played in the NBA.

Casey has done neither. Still, as of late he remained hopeful.

"There's a window of opportunity," he says. "You have to be at the right time and place and be prepared, which I think I am. In the meantime, one of my 'isms' is to do the best job I can at the place I am, and I'm with the Sonics. As far as being a head coach in the NBA? I haven't given up hope."

But Casey has given up other things. The bitterness, the anger from the Emery incident? Those are gone.

There are reasons.

Casey remains friends with Chris Mills, Claude Mills and Harvey Kitani. He's also close to several former Kentucky coaches, in particular ex-assistant Leonard Hamilton, whom he used to visit with all the time when Hamilton was coaching the NBA's Washington Wizards.

Those friendships have helped, but two occurrences in the early 1990s also accelerated Casey's healing. First, Emery agreed with Casey that he had been unfairly maligned by the company's employee and settled a lawsuit Casey had brought. Second, three years into his five-year probation, the NCAA set Casey free. Look at those two facts in tandem, and it looks an awful lot like an exoneration.

Today, Casey can't remember the name of the Emery employee who ruined his college coaching career. Even though he spent several days sitting across a table from the young man during the deposition-taking stage of his lawsuit, Casey can't even picture the guy's face.

"I never dreamed that would be possible," says Casey.

Other things also seem impossible. In 1990, Dwane Casey was out of work, wondering if he would ever coach again. Within a decade he would be an established assistant, one who would be invited to interview for five head coaching jobs in the NBA—the pinnacle of basketball?

"I never dreamed it could happen," he says. "To be very honest with you, if you told me [in 1990] I'd be in this position, I'd have said you're crazy. I wouldn't have believed that for a million dollars."

How about two million? That's how much money Casey was set to earn in the 2005-06 NBA season with the Minnesota Timberwolves—who hired him as head coach on June 17, 2005.

Some small acts of kindness pay *big*.

Where Have You Gone?

BILL SPIVEY

One-half of the greatest player in Kentucky basketball history floats in the Atlantic Ocean.

The other half of Bill Spivey was supposed to float in the Pacific, according to his final wishes. But he never got his wish. Instead, Spivey's family sprinkled all of his cremated remains into the Atlantic, off the coast of South Carolina.

Typical. Spivey didn't get exactly what he wanted in life. Why should death have been any different?

"I wanted to get out there [to the Pacific Ocean]," says Spivey's son, Cashton, a psychologist who lives in Charleston, S.C. "I could only do so much. I hope he'd be okay with that."

What does it matter? Life didn't go according to Spivey's plan, either.

Most Kentucky fans know all about Spivey's days on campus, when he became the school's first seven-footer in 1949 and led the Wildcats to a national championship in 1951. They know all about the end of his college playing days, when he was mistakenly implicated in the nationwide point-shaving scandal that cost Kentucky the 1952-53 season and unfairly cost Spivey his senior season and NBA career.

But few people know the rest of the story, the 44 years Spivey lived after the scandal. They were 44 painful years.

"He was bitter about the whole thing," says former teammate Lou Tsioropoulos, a forward on Kentucky's 1951 championship team. "He was very bitter. It bothered him his whole life."

With good reason, probably. While only Spivey knows exactly what he did or didn't do, the evidence overwhelmingly points to the conclusion that

BILL SPIVEY

Years lettered: 1949-50, 1950-51
Honors: All-SEC and All-American, 1950-51; All-SEC 1949-50;
retired jersey No. 77
Career totals: 1,213 points (32nd in UK history), 17.2 rebounding average in 1950-51, school-record 34 rebounds
in a single game in 1950-51

he was an innocent victim of the worst point-shaving scandal of his era. To his death, Spivey denied involvement in the scandal that took down former Kentucky teammates Ralph Beard and Alex Groza, who were budding NBA stars in 1951 when they were banned from the league.

For Beard and Groza, the punishment might have been just. They admitted receiving money—thought to be $500 each—from gamblers to shave points during a loss to Loyola Chicago in the 1949 National Invitation Tournament. They were later given suspended sentences in court and placed on indefinite probation.

For Spivey, the evidence shows that the punishment didn't fit the crime—because there was no crime. Spivey was never tried for point shaving, and he avoided conviction in his only trial, a perjury charge after prosecutors accused him of lying about his role in the scandal. The jury deadlocked at 9-3 in favor of acquittal before the case was dismissed.

None of that mattered to the men in charge of NCAA and NBA basketball. Spivey was ruled ineligible for his senior season in 1951-52, surely costing the 29-3 Wildcats, who lost in the second round of the NCAA Tournament, another national championship.

It was an even bigger heartbreak—and a bigger travesty—when the court case was resolved in Spivey's favor and NBA commissioner Maurice Podoloff still blacklisted him from the NBA. Instead of joining the likes of George Mikan and Bob Pettit as the premier NBA players of his era, Spivey was relegated to minor-league basketball for nearly two decades before retiring at age 38.

"The little emperor, Maurice Podoloff, and his buddies had control of the NBA," says Tsioropoulos. "They couldn't keep Bill out of the NBA now. Connie Hawkins sued [in the late 1960s] and got to play in the NBA, but at the time they could do whatever they wanted. And the NBA turned its back on Bill Spivey."

The highest level of basketball may have turned its back on Spivey, but Spivey couldn't turn his back on basketball. And in the mid-1950s he had plenty of other options. The NBA was a small league with just nine teams, and international basketball wasn't a viable option for most Americans. That left a lot of fine U.S. basketball players to fend for themselves, which led to a handful of other leagues and opportunities. Spivey took advantage.

Spivey's first two professional teams were the Detroit Vagabonds and Boston Whirlwinds, fateful nicknames for a player who would play on six barnstorming teams, many in the Harlem Globetrotters' organization, before playing for five franchises in two U.S. minor leagues—the Eastern Basketball League and the American Basketball League. During his time in the Globetrotters' system, Spivey was involved in a fight with Bobby "Showboat" Hall during a game in Australia.

Along the way, Spivey sued the NBA for $800,000 in compensation for lost wages. He settled that case for $10,000. By the late 1960s he was still playing professionally, earning roughly $200 a game for Wilkes-Barre of the Eastern League. By then Spivey was in his late 30s, good enough to average 10.4 points per game but far from the dominant player he had been in his prime. In an earlier tour with Wilkes-Barre, Spivey averaged 36 points over the 1959 and 1960 seasons, with high games of 64 and 62 points. This wasn't the NBA, but it was real basketball with real talent. Players in the old EBL included Hawkins, a future NBA star; Bill Sharman was among the coaches.

Still, for a player of Spivey's talent, it wasn't enough. Nearly anyone who saw him play in his prime insists Spivey would have been one of the all-time greats. In college he tore up Kansas All-American Clyde Lovellette, outscoring the future Hall of Famer 22 to 10 in a Kentucky victory in December 1950. Spivey capped that season by putting up 22 points and 21 rebounds on Kansas State's Lew Hitch, who would spend six years in the NBA. That came in the 1951 NCAA championship game, a Kentucky victory and Spivey's final game of college.

Spivey's legend grew from there, even as he played in under-the-radar leagues. There's the story of him practicing during the 1959-60 season with the NBA's Cincinnati Royals and tearing up Royals center Wayne Embry, a double-double scorer-rebounder for most of that decade. There's the story of him dropping 44 points on Connie Dierking, another future NBA stalwart, in an EBL game in 1962. And there's the story of a 1960 exhibition at Milford, Connecticut, in which Spivey had 30 points and 23 rebounds but was outdone by his counterpart, who had 31 points and 27 rebounds. No shame in that—his counterpart was Wilt Chamberlain.

"There's no way to know for sure," says former Kentucky coach Joe B. Hall. "However, most people feel [Spivey] would have been one of the top five centers of all-time had he had the chance to mature in the NBA."

By age 40, Spivey was physically broken. His ankle and knees were devastated from two decades of basketball, and his back was in bad shape. He returned to Kentucky for various business ventures, mostly in sales, though he owned a couple of restaurants for a time, too.

"He did all right," says Spivey's son, Cash. "For the time, he was probably middle class."

Spivey also sold insurance and became Kentucky's deputy state insurance commissioner. In 1983 he announced his candidacy for lieutenant governor, but nothing came of it. By 1991 he was a recluse, returning to the public eye only once more—and grudgingly at that. It took calls from several team-mates to get Spivey back to Lexington in 1991 for the 40th reunion of the 1951 championship team.

By then Spivey was living in Daytona Beach, Florida, where his life took what was eventually a tragic turn in a car accident.

"He was going through an intersection and a woman ran a red light and significantly re-injured his former lower-back injury," Cash Spivey says. "This time he was hurt to the point where he had to have bone grafts. He never really made a full recovery from that. It affected his posture, and he had chronic pain from that."

It didn't help that doctors may have botched the procedure. According to Spivey's son, a small piece of surgical equipment—a "probe," Cash Spivey says—was broken off in Spivey's back. There it remained for the rest of his life, a secret until a future X-ray revealed the foreign object in his lower back. Bill Spivey sued the hospital and won a small reward, Cash Spivey says.

"But it wasn't like it gave him a better life," the son says. "It covered some of his medical fees, and that's about it. It wasn't worth the suffering he went through."

In 1993, Spivey joined a friend on a trip to Costa Rica and fell in love with the Central American country. He began taking Spanish lessons in Daytona Beach, and six months later he moved to Quepos, a small coastal town on the Pacific Ocean side of Costa Rica. Spivey's wife, Audrey, stayed behind, though there wasn't a divorce or even a legal separation. It was just another odd step in the odd life of Bill Spivey.

"He took a suitcase, and he was gone," Cash Spivey says. "It surprised me a little. I thought he was going to a poverty-stricken, third-world country. But, it's a beautiful place, and they do love Americans. I visited him twice down there and totally understood. His quote of Costa Rica was something like this: 'Costa Rica was Hawaii in the 1950s before we Americans ruined it.'"

Part of the allure for Costa Rica, located between Nicaragua and Panama, was its economy. The dollar lasted longer there than it did in Florida, and by 1994 Spivey needed to stretch his money. He was no longer able to work, and he was in constant need of medication for back pain as well as respiratory issues stemming from congestive heart failure.

By 1995, Spivey had broken down physically. That spring Cash Spivey sent his father a package of medicine, but when the overnight package went unacknowledged, Cash called his father's landlord.

"That's when I learned he was deceased," Cash says.

On May 8, 1995, authorities had found Spivey in his apartment, dead of natural causes. He was 66.

Two weeks later Spivey was remembered during a 30-minute ceremony at a Main Street funeral home in Lexington. Close to 60 people attended. With luck, they heard the following story from Tsioropoulos, who remembers his former teammate as "a gentle giant who'd do anything for you."

"In the 1970s I got my back operated on," Tsioropoulos says. "I was supposed to get out of bed three times a day, but I couldn't do it. I was living in Louisville and so was Bill, and he found out about me because [my wife] Jan called his wife, Audrey. He came that night. He said, 'I'll be there.'"

At the time, Spivey was in his 40s and in constant back pain himself. At six foot five and close to 200 pounds, Tsioropoulos was no small man. The in-home nurse assigned to Tsioropoulos couldn't pick him up. Enter Spivey.

"Bill came every morning and picked me up out of bed," Tsioropoulos says. "Then he went to work and came back in mid-afternoon to get me out of bed again. Then he came back at night. He'd put arms right under me and pick me up and put me on my feet."

Kentucky retired Spivey's No. 77 jersey in January 2000. The ceremony came at the urging of then-Wildcats athletics director C.M. Newton, Spivey's roommate in college. Four years later Spivey was inducted into the Kentucky Sports Hall of Fame. His widow, Audrey, gave the speech.

"I'm so nervous," she said two days before the September 2004 ceremony. "But I'm happy for Bill. He would have seen all of these things (the jersey, the hall of fame) as vindication in the eyes of the university and the state. That would have meant the world to him."

Where Have You Gone?

ADOLPH RUPP

First, he was a basketball coach, and a damn good one. Then, he was a prophet who predicted the circumstances of his own death. Unfortunately, he was good at that, too.

Now, Adolph Rupp has become a tourist attraction.

Where—to borrow the title from this book—has Rupp gone? Nowhere—at least not since December 10, 1977. That's when the curmudgeonly old coach made his last trip, from University Medical Center on the University of Kentucky campus to The Lexington Cemetery, a few miles west on Main Street.

Rupp had very little privacy in life, and in death it has been no different. The Lexington Cemetery offers a brochure for visitors to its 170-acre grounds. The brochure pinpoints the exact location of 13 burial sites out of more than 63,000 interments.

One is Henry Clay, the 19th-century statesman and senator from Kentucky. He's located in Section M. Another is John C. Breckinridge, the 13th and still youngest vice president in U.S. history who unsuccessfully tried to beat Abraham Lincoln in the 1860 presidential election. He's located in Section G.

And then there's the old coach himself, Adolph F. Rupp, located in Section 45 between the Gardens of Tranquility, Peace and Consolation.

According to an employee of Lexington Cemetery, the location of Rupp's grave wasn't always on the brochure. But over time its addition became a necessity. Just inside the gate sits the cemetery's offices, where visitors come seeking directions to Rupp's grave. The most traffic arrives in the spring, when the state high school basketball tournament is held in Lexington, and

ADOLPH RUPP

Head coach: 1930-72
Honors: Naismith Basketball Hall of Fame, 1969; 1959, 1966
national coach of the year; retired jersey (no number)
Career totals: 876-190; wins are second all-time in NCAA
Division I; 1948, 1949, 1951 and 1958 NCAA championships;
1948 Olympic gold medal

many of its participants—coaches, players and their families—make the small sojourn down Main Street from Rupp Arena to Rupp's grave.

It's a beautiful location. There are more than 200 species of trees on the grounds, and the trees that surround Rupp's grave are leafy and enormous.

This is where Rupp knew he'd be, and he even knew roughly when he'd get here. It was during the 1971-72 season when Rupp was fighting for his job after reaching the state's mandatory retirement age of 70. Winning four national championships and 27 SEC titles wasn't about to buy him an extra season, and amid the controversy about his future Rupp uttered the famous words, "If they don't let me coach, they might as well take me to the Lexington Cemetery."

Indeed, Rupp's health had been deteriorating during his final years on the Kentucky bench. In 1970 he spent weeks at a time in bed, leaving his house only for practice, games and trips to the doctor. Early in the 1969-70 season he took up two seats on the bench, using one chair to prop up his foot.

Rupp was diagnosed with diabetes, a condition he kept mostly to himself. By the time the Wildcats moved into brand-new Rupp Arena in November 1976, Rupp could rarely visit the building bearing his name. The school had erected a blue velvet chair for Rupp, but it usually went unfilled.

Adolph Rupp was dying. Cancer of the spine along with diabetes was ending his life, and on Nov. 9, 1977, Rupp was admitted to University Medical Center. He was dead 31 days later, at age 76. Kentucky Gov. Julian Carroll declared December 10, 1977 to be a day of mourning and ordered flags to fly at half-staff.

Rupp's gravesite is noticeable but not ostentatious. In a cemetery that has scores of gaudy tombstones reaching 30 feet into the air and a handful of miniature mausoleums devoted to people who, frankly, don't need all that room, Rupp's tombstone is classy. It is roughly three feet wide and eight feet tall, with a basketball carved into the stone. Below that are these words, and only these words:

ADOLPH FREDERICK RUPP
U.K. BASKETBALL COACH 42 YEARS
OLYMPIC COACH 1948
FOUR NCAA CHAMPIONSHIPS
NATIONAL BASKETBALL HALL OF FAME

In front of the tombstone, set into the ground about six inches apart, are two shoebox-sized markers for the actual gravesites of Rupp and his widow. Esther Rupp died March 29, 1998, another passing that dominated state headlines. Former Wildcat Larry Pursiful, an ordained minister, officiated at her funeral.

Nearby is the gravesite of Rupp's longtime assistant coach, Harry Lancaster. After coaching alongside Rupp for 22 years, Lancaster became Kentucky's athletics director—and Rupp's boss—in 1969. Three years later, when Rupp was forced to retire at age 70, many Kentucky fans—and reportedly Rupp himself—blamed Lancaster for not being able to stop it. The two men didn't speak much over the next several years but had made amends before Rupp's death.

Now Lancaster is buried two plots behind Rupp and off to the left, almost looking over the Baron's shoulder.

That's one thing a visitor will notice upon visiting Rupp's grave. And visitors still come, almost 30 years after his death.

Another thing a visitor might notice is the name on a nearby tombstone, a tombstone one must pass before being able to get an eyeful of the tourist attraction that is Rupp's last home.

The tombstone has a name on it: Ogle.

Where Have You Gone?

TRUMAN CLAYTOR

I t happens when Truman Claytor is in the grocery store, or at the bank, or walking through the mall. A young man will approach with a smile on his mouth and recognition in his eyes. Claytor is still something of a legend around Toledo thanks to his high school exploits, not to mention his role as a shooting guard on Kentucky's 1978 national championship team.

But when it happens, it's bigger than basketball. These young men don't want to talk hoops. They want to thank Claytor—*thank you*—for helping fix their broken lives.

"That's when it's all worth it," says Claytor, who counsels adolescent addicts for a rehabilitation center in Toledo, Ohio. "It's an uphill battle sometimes, because there is so much denial, but then somebody will walk up to me and say, 'You remember me, Mr. Claytor? You saved my life.'"

Claytor knows how they feel. He has been working as a counselor since 1989, but the passage of time doesn't dull his own painful memories of addiction or the joy that comes with liberation.

Addiction snuck up on Claytor.

It started small, with some alcohol while he was in college. At the time drinking was legal for an 18-year-old, and as long as Claytor didn't drink during the season, there was nothing the Kentucky coaching staff could do about it. Eventually, though, Claytor moved on to marijuana. He was on the road to addiction, already in too deep to recognize his chance to get clean while still in college.

"I got caught smoking pot one time [by the coaches], and after that I couldn't smoke any more in the season," he says. "But after the season, I went back to smoking and drinking."

TRUMAN CLAYTOR

Years lettered: 1975-76, 1976-77, 1977-78, 1978-79
Career totals: 821 points, 117 rebounds, 213 assists

Claytor finished his Kentucky career with two SEC championships and an NIT title to go with that 1978 national championship ring. He scored 821 career points and was drafted in the sixth round in 1979 by the Detroit Pistons. The Pistons cut Claytor that fall, and the Philadelphia 76ers cut him the following fall. This was 1980, after the demise of the old American Basketball Association but before the advent of various minor leagues in the United States.

Claytor was finished with basketball. But not finished with drugs.

He returned to Toledo where he embarked on a series of jobs—for the phone company, or selling life insurance, or getting work through a temp agency—while continuing to drink and smoke marijuana. In 1983, Claytor was at a party when someone introduced him to cocaine.

Eventually Claytor was turned on to crack. To this day he remembers vividly the point when he hit rock bottom. He can still see the look on his mother's face early that morning in 1987, after a night of partying with a friend, when she came into the living room and saw that her color television set was gone.

At three o'clock that morning, Claytor and his friend had carried the TV out the front door. They sold it for $50, which they used to buy more crack.

"I came back at 5 a.m., and my mother woke up and looked at me," Claytor says. "I couldn't even look at her. I tried to look at her in the eyes, and I saw the hurt and disappointment she saw in me, and that was it. That was my bottom. I went and got help."

By 1989, Claytor had been clean for two years. He was working as a substitute teacher in the Toledo public school system, attending regular meetings for recovering addicts, when he learned about an opening for an adolescent counselor at Toledo Hospital.

"I was excited," he says. "I was really excited and blessed to be able to have that opportunity to even have a job. Here I was recovering, and trying to treat the addiction myself, and now I had gotten a chance to help others with their addiction."

Claytor applied for the job and got it. At first he had to learn to compartmentalize his life into two areas: Taking care of Truman and taking care of others.

"I had to put my 'recovery' hat on when I left the door," Claytor says, "but put on my 'work' hat when I got to the hospital."

Sometimes, though, he wears both hats at the same time. There is something powerful in the counsel of one who has experienced the same depths as an addict, and Claytor uses his story to show his patients that recovery isn't just a dream. It can be reality.

It helps, too, that Claytor remains a well-known name in Toledo's basketball community, and that many of the kids who are brought to him for help belong to that community. The ones who don't know about Claytor's basketball exploits can be taught by a glance at his NCAA title ring, or a picture of him in his No. 22 Kentucky jersey, elevating for one of his textbook jumpers.

"That opens their eyes up and puts their defenses down a little bit," he says. "I use that every once in a while. Some of the kids come in and they're talented artists. I might take down my picture from playing basketball and have them draw it."

Claytor is still involved in basketball. He has been refereeing college games at the Division II and Division III levels since the early 1990s, and has attended various Division I camps in the summer. He'd like to break into officiating at the Division I level, but the competition for those positions is as competitive as scholarships and coaching jobs.

In the meantime, Claytor officiates small college and high school games, and also works with another Toledo basketball legend, former 76ers forward Steve Mix, at clinics. Occasionally the parent of a camper will pull Claytor aside after a session and ask if he does any private shooting instruction.

Absolutely, Claytor says.

"I enjoy teaching kids to shoot," he says. "I could always shoot the ball."

There are some things you never get over.

And there are some things, Truman Claytor has learned, you do.

Where Have You Gone?

TOM PAYNE

O nly Tom Payne knows how much hatred he endured as the first black player in Kentucky basketball history. Tragically, the rest of us can see what that hatred did to him.

Payne, a seven-foot-two center, broke Kentucky's color barrier in 1970-71 when he averaged 16.9 points and 10.1 rebounds. After that season he declared for the NBA's 1971 Hardship Draft. He left behind one form of hatred but soon he would discover another.

By 1977 he was in prison, where he has spent much of his adult life for a series of sex-crime convictions. For years he has been incarcerated at a medium-security facility in southwest Kentucky, having been convicted of two counts of kidnapping and one count of rape. He's not eligible for parole until October 2014, the year he turns 64.

Payne did not speak to the author of this book. Interview requests were made through various officials at Green River Correctional Complex in Central City, Kentucky, but none were granted. It wasn't clear whether Payne even received the requests. Call after call to prison officials went unreturned.

Intensive searches on the Internet and other resources produced only one known interview with Payne. It was found on the official web site of the National Association of Black Coaches, in a story by reporter Mike Douchant about players who had broken color barriers in college basketball.

In the story, which was published on an unidentified date in the 1990s, Douchant reported that Payne had dealt with "threatening phone calls, broken car windows and eggs smashed on his front door."

TOM PAYNE

Years lettered: 1970-71
Honors: All-SEC 1970-71
Career totals: 473 points, 283 rebounds, 16 assists

"That's the kind of abuse I went through," Payne was quoted as saying by Douchant. "And people think that's not supposed to affect you? Before I went to college, nothing in my life said I was going to be a criminal. My whole life took a turn going to UK and getting damaged so much. My anger and hatred toward white society came up, and I lashed out."

Indeed, there were no known instances of criminal behavior by Payne before he signed with Kentucky coach Adolph Rupp in 1969. (Payne sat out the 1969-70 season while getting academically eligible.) At Kentucky he experienced things no teammate had ever had to face, including a racial epithet scrawled on the chalkboard in the visiting locker room at Tennessee. During that January 16, 1971 game at Tennessee, where the Volunteers' basketball team hadn't yet been desegregated, Payne was the subject of such brutal booing that Kentucky teammates Mike Casey and Larry Steele told game officials the Wildcats would walk off the court if it didn't stop.

Steele remembers the stress that Payne was under, but he also remembers how Rupp tried to alleviate that stress.

"Coach Rupp seemed to go out of his way to make sure Tom, initially at least, had a smooth transition from high school to college," Steele says. "As everyone knows, Coach Rupp was extremely difficult on players—extremely difficult. It was tough, tough, tough to play for Coach Rupp, but he seemed to try to take some of that pressure off Tom, because everyone was well aware of the scrutiny the basketball program was under at the time."

Only Tom Payne knows exactly what it felt like to cross that historic line at such a sensitive time and place in the United States.

However, Perry Wallace knows something about what Payne went through. And Wallace says Payne's criminal response to that stress is inexcusable.

Hear him out. Wallace offers a unique perspective on Tom Payne for two reasons.

First, Wallace broke the Southeastern Conference's color barrier for basketball at Vanderbilt, doing so in 1967—three years before Payne would play for Kentucky. He went into those same SEC gyms and experienced the same hatred.

Second, Wallace has been a law professor at The American University in Washington D.C. since 1991. He is a former attorney with the U.S. Department of Justice, meaning he has been in the kinds of courtrooms that would one day claim Tom Payne's freedom.

As a black man in a white sport in the South, Wallace says the hate he experienced was so thick, so vile, that he might not have signed with Vanderbilt had he known what lay ahead.

The integrationist in Wallace sympathizes with Payne's anger, but the jurist in Wallace despises how Payne expressed that anger.

"In my class I often talk about the difference between a reason and an excuse," Wallace says. "The racism [Payne] encountered, some of the things I dealt with, might be a reason or an explanation for what he did later—but they don't provide you with an excuse to go out and behave that way.

"Lord knows I've read about Tom Payne and I don't want to sound like I'm unsympathetic. My heart really hurts as I read about his difficulty, and I felt like I was uniquely able to understand some of the forces that engulfed him. But what I also understood from my own experience is there's a unique battle for your own soul, and you have to win the battle for your soul."

According to various reports, Payne was a three-time loser, convicted of rape or similar crimes in three states—eventually violating his parole on a life sentence. That's how he ended up at Green River Correctional, a 982-bed facility that opened in 1994. In late 2004, Green River records showed the facility was filled just beyond capacity, with a capacity of 947 inmates but a population of 956. And it was filled with a particularly dangerous brand of inmate. According to state records, 67 percent of the inmates were incarcerated because of violent or sexual crimes.

That population included one very large, very talented former Kentucky player. Had Payne stayed at Kentucky for two more seasons, he could have grown into a dominant NBA center. When Rupp was recruiting Payne, the old Kentucky coach told Payne's father—a retired Army sergeant—that the younger Payne was better at age 18 than legendary Kentucky seven-footer Bill Spivey had been two decades earlier. As if it needs to be said, the cantankerous Rupp wasn't prone to blowing smoke up anyone's britches.

After sitting out the 1969-70 season, Payne started quickly in 1970-71. He posted double-doubles (in his case at least 10 points and 10 rebounds) in five of his first six games, including a 19-point, 19-rebound game against West Virginia and an 18-point, 19-rebound performance against DePaul.

By the end of the season Payne was the team's most dominant player. He had 34 points and 15 rebounds in a mid-February win against Georgia, then topped that five days later with 39 points and 19 rebounds in a win against Louisiana State. In the Wildcats' March 1 victory against Auburn that sealed their SEC title and NCAA bid, Payne had 30 points and 12 rebounds.

Payne's final game was a disaster, though. In the Wildcats' season-ending loss to Marquette in the 1971 NCAA Tournament, Payne fouled out. He had one point and one rebound. Weeks later he would declare for the NBA draft.

Of the five players selected in the now-defunct hardship phase of the draft, Payne was taken second by the Atlanta Hawks. He spent just one season in the NBA, averaging 4.1 points and 2.4 rebounds in 29 games. Steele was playing with the Portland Trailblazers that season, and he remembers a game in Atlanta on December 27, 1971.

"When I came into the gym before the game, all the Hawks were at one end," Steele says. "Tom yelled at me, turned to his teammates and said, 'This was the only guy I could trust at the University of Kentucky.' It's just unfortunate."

By then, according to Kentucky Department of Corrections records, Payne already had committed his first rape. The department makes available certain information about each of its inmates on the Internet, and the web page devoted to Payne indicates he raped a woman on September 4, 1971 but wasn't convicted until September 1977. Payne's web page lists his official height and weight at 7-1, 290 pounds. The face in the mug has bloodshot eyes. Payne looks angry, defeated.

Wallace, the Vanderbilt pioneer, wishes Payne had found another way of dealing with his anger.

"[He was] engaged in the battle of being a pioneer at Kentucky or in the SEC, as I was, and that's one big struggle," Wallace says. "But the other aspect of it is what I call 'struggling well.' You don't let the negativity or the evil around you get the best of you. If the environment tries to kill a person, you don't finish the job. That environment will foist on you feelings of rage and hatred, but if you go for that, it will destroy you. What will happen is you'll go off and destroy yourself."

Where Have You Gone?

DEREK
SMITH

A hotshot high school athlete could learn something from Derek Smith. A hotshot college athlete could learn even more. Derek Smith has learned plenty along the way, and his journey isn't finished. Not even close. Remember the name, because he's going to make his mark in professional sports.

Even if it's not the mark everyone expected when he was the most celebrated two-sport athlete in recent Kentucky Wildcats history.

Smith's not going to play in the NBA, though he once finished second in Kentucky's Mr. Basketball voting and had all of Kentucky Basketball Nation excited about his presence in Rupp Arena. Smith's also not going to the NFL, though he was an All-SEC tight end at Kentucky and spent time on the Cincinnati Bengals' practice squad.

Once a wildly famous teenage prodigy in three sports, the year 2005 found Smith toiling under the radar at Northern Kentucky University, an almost completely bald 24-year-old power forward for an NCAA Division II powerhouse. The hair had succumbed to genetics, not stress, though there has been plenty of stress. There also has been rumor and innuendo, questions raised but never answered.

Smith is ready to answer those questions now. He's ready to share his story, and it's a good one.

First, there are rumors to be addressed concerning both of Smith's former football coaches at Kentucky, the defrocked Hal Mumme (who was fired by Kentucky and then started over at Southeastern Louisiana) and the exalted Guy Morriss (who bolted Kentucky for Baylor after the 2002 season).

One rumor had it—on good authority, mind you—that Mumme had reneged on a recruiting promise to let Smith play two sports for the

DEREK SMITH

Years lettered (football only): 1999, 2000, 2001
Honors: All-SEC tight end, 2000

Wildcats, dashing Smith's lifelong dream of playing Kentucky basketball. That rumor was so rampant that the state's best high school athlete in 2002, Michael Bush, asked colleges to put in writing that he could play two sports. Two years later Bush was playing football only at Louisville.

Another rumor had it—on good authority, you understand—that Morriss, who replaced Mumme before Smith's junior season, clashed repeatedly with Smith and was going to redshirt him in 2002. Which is why Smith unexpectedly entered the 2002 NFL Draft as a junior.

Only one rumor, Smith says, is true. And it's not the one you'd expect.

"[Mumme] never told me I couldn't play basketball," he says. "That was my decision."

Smith had planned to play basketball for Kentucky. And Kentucky coach Tubby Smith planned to have him—even ordering a "D. Smith" jersey (to go with the "S. Smith" the Kentucky coach had ordered for his son, guard Saul Smith).

But football was an issue. Derek Smith had nine catches as a Wildcats freshman reserve in 1999, two more than fellow freshman Bobby Blizzard. They were set to compete for the starting job in 2000, and Blizzard was committed to spending that spring preparing for the battle.

"No one told me if I played basketball I was going to fall behind [Blizzard]. No one had to—I knew," Smith says. "I didn't just want to be a [football] contributor. I wanted to be *the* guy, so I spent the spring lifting and getting ready. That was my choice. And it wasn't like I was going to have much of a role on the basketball team. Look at me."

Smith has a point. He's six foot five, 250 pounds. He looks like an All-SEC tight end. He also looks like a Division II power forward.

Skipping basketball paid off. Smith beat out Blizzard—who later transferred to North Carolina and earned All-ACC honors—and caught 50 passes in 2000. He caught 30 more in 2001 under Morriss.

And then? Well, yes, Morriss talked to Smith about redshirting in 2002. As you could imagine, Smith wasn't receptive.

"At the time I was so crazy when he told me about redshirting that I didn't see he was looking out for my best interests," Smith says. "Now I see it. My body needed more time to get ready [for the NFL], but I was 21. I'm 24 now, and it's only three years, but you mature. You see things differently."

Knowing what he knows now, Smith says he'd probably do things differently. No, he wouldn't have played basketball for Kentucky. He feels he was on the money when he gave up that sport to concentrate on football. But if he could go back, he'd probably redshirt that 2002 season instead of entering the draft. He went undrafted, then was a late cut in the Indianapolis Colts' training camp in 2002. He spent part of that season on the Bengals' practice squad but was released without game action. The St. Louis Rams invited him to training camp in early 2004, but Smith declined. It was time to move on.

Smith left Lexington without a degree, something he planned to rectify at Northern Kentucky. The 14,000-student school offers a degree in sports business, which Smith hopes to use in pro sports—perhaps in salary-cap issues or in helping athletes manage money.

When he returned to college, basketball wasn't part of the deal. Smith had earned money from the Bengals and Colts, and besides, his five-year NCAA "clock" had expired with the 2003-04 school year. He had no eligibility left. Or so he thought.

Smith enrolled at Northern Kentucky in August 2004 with no fanfare, but when one of the all-time scoring leaders in Kentucky high school basketball enrolls at your college, the basketball program hears about it. Smith had scored 2,299 points at Highlands High in Fort Thomas, Kentucky. Northern Kentucky assistant Pat Ryan heard about it.

As it turns out, Smith had college eligibility galore in any sport but football. As for Smith's five-year window, that applied only to Division I. As far as NCAA Division II was concerned, Smith entered the 2004-05 school year with five semesters of eligibility. That's almost three complete seasons of college basketball.

"I couldn't believe it," Smith says. "I wasn't [at Northern Kentucky] to play basketball, but I thought, 'Maybe I should do this. Here's another chance.'"

This kind of athletic ability would be a shame to waste. Smith also pitched in high school, hitting 94 miles an hour on one Major League Baseball scout's radar gun. When Smith quit after his sophomore season, a scout with the Milwaukee Brewers called to ask why—then asked Smith if the Brewers should spend a draft pick on him in 1999. Don't bother, Smith said.

And baseball was his third best sport.

The Hoop Scoop basketball recruiting service ranked Smith as the country's No. 78 high school senior in 1999, one spot ahead of future Georgia star Ezra Williams and two spots ahead of Cincinnati's Tony Bobbitt.

And basketball was his second best sport.

In November 2004 Smith made his Northern Kentucky debut, his first organized basketball game since 1999. Guess where: Rupp Arena. Northern Kentucky happened to be Kentucky's exhibition opener, and in 16 minutes against All-America candidate Chuck Hayes, Smith had five points and five rebounds.

"It was great to be back," Smith says. "It wasn't the first time I played there [he also had played in Rupp in high school, during the boys state tournament], but it was great to come out and compete."

An infected blister sidelined Smith for Northern Kentucky's next exhibition game, at the University of Cincinnati, but that didn't stop a fan from spending most of the second half yelling, "Derek Smith for president!"

Where Have You Gone?

DERRICK MILLER

Derrick Miller made a promise to Tubby Smith, and while it took him more than a decade to get it done, Miller wanted to be a man of his word.

Smith was a Kentucky assistant coach under Rick Pitino in 1990, and Miller was the senior ringleader of "Pitino's Bombinos." That spring Miller had a chance to play professionally in Argentina, but he hadn't graduated yet. Before taking off for South America, he promised Smith to return to school some day and get his degree.

Twelve years later Miller was back at Kentucky thanks to the Cawood Ledford Scholarship Fund, named for the former voice of the Wildcats. Taking a class or two at a time, Miller was on pace to graduate in the spring of 2005 at age 37.

Best part of the story? Smith also had come back to Kentucky, returning as head coach in 1997 following stints at Tulsa and Georgia. Not counting family members, the first person on Miller's graduation invitation list was Smith.

"We're still pretty close," Miller says. "I made him that promise, and after he came back [as head coach] I told him I was going to stick to it."

A loyal guy, Derrick Miller—but then, he'd proved that a long time ago. Back in 1989, when the world was caving in on Kentucky basketball and players were fleeing like rats from a sinking ship, Miller was one of the handful of scholarship players who stuck it out. After an NCAA investigation that led to sanctions, probation and the dismissal of coach Eddie Sutton, leading scorers LeRon Ellis and Chris Mills took off for Syracuse and Arizona, respectively. Point guard Sean Sutton, Eddie's son, transferred

DERRICK MILLER

Years lettered: 1986-87, 1987-88, 1988-89, 1989-90
Honors: All-SEC 1989-90
Career totals: 1,156 points (36th in UK history), 269 rebounds,
125 assists, 191 three-pointers (2nd in UK history)

to Oklahoma State. Mike Scott, a reserve center who was one of just five Wildcats to play in every game in 1988-89, lit out for Wake Forest.

The exodus left behind a core of young players—Richie Farmer, Deron Feldhaus, John Pelphrey and Sean Woods—who would become known as "The Unforgettables." And it left behind Miller, who wasn't around for the magical 1992 season and wonders if along the way he became The Forgotten.

"The fans remember, but sometimes I'm not sure the school does," Miller says. "I was the first guy who stayed. I stayed at UK when just about everyone else [among the upperclassmen] left. They talk about The Unforgettables, but that was after me. Guys like Reggie Hanson and I were the oldest guys who stayed, and sometimes that's missed. But that's neither here nor there. I'm not bitter about it."

Definitely not. Miller remains one of Kentucky's most loyal ambassadors, a guy who literally goes door to door throughout the state, drumming up interest in Kentucky basketball. He and another unsung ex-Wildcat, point guard Ed Davender, work for a private company called Kentucky Sports History that chronicles each season of UK hoops into one fan-friendly book and then donates copies of that book to schools around the state. To pay the bills, Miller and Davender sell sponsorships and advertisements to businesses who want to appear in the book.

On a typical day of work, Miller will drive to a school somewhere in the state—could be down the street, could be 300 miles away—with two purposes. One, he'll drop off copies of the previous season's book and occasionally make a speech about saying yes to Kentucky basketball and saying no to drugs. Two, he'll visit area businesses to find sponsors for the following year's book.

"It's fun, real fun," Miller says. "I put 30,000 miles on my car every year, easily. I've been to every county in the state, and the whole state likes Kentucky basketball. Eastern Kentucky, western Kentucky—it's not split up. You go to Louisville and they might like both teams, but anywhere else you go, they like Kentucky."

And a lot of them remember Miller.

"I can go to Paducah, Clinton, they know Derrick Miller," he says. "These are people who don't get to go to Rupp Arena for games, but they know Kentucky basketball, and they remember me."

For even a casual student of Kentucky basketball, Miller would be pretty tough to forget. He was the original Pitino Bombino, leading the Wildcats in scoring as a senior at 19.2 points per game and chucking three-pointers at a rate never seen at Kentucky—before or since. His 289 three-point attempts that season set a school record that might stand the test of time, as did the 19 three-pointers he attempted in a game at Kansas. In the latter category, Miller holds the top seven spots in the UK record book—attempting at least 15 three-pointers in seven different games.

Along the way Miller became the first Kentucky player to score 40 points at Rupp Arena, reaching that mark as a senior against Vanderbilt, a game that he broke open with six three-pointers in the second half.

With Miller doing the heaviest lifting, Pitino's first season was a surprising success—or at least a surprising lack of failure. After the Wildcats had gone 13-19 the previous season in Eddie Sutton's last year, Pitino's first team that was depleted by those four transfers was predicted to win less than 10 games. The Wildcats instead went a respectable 14-14, setting the foundation for the glory years to come when the Wildcats won 22 games in 1991 and 29 games in 1992.

Miller was long gone by then, having set out for Argentina and a four-year career there. He returned to the United States in the mid-1990s to play one season in the Continental Basketball Association, then retired.

Miller has stayed in the game by working for Kentucky Sports History and through attending Kentucky practices to visit with Smith and Hanson, his former roommate and now an assistant coach.

"I've got to keep up with the team," Miller says. "When I go out on the road, people want to talk Kentucky basketball. I better have something to tell them."

Where Have You Gone?

BRET
BEARUP

He might be the most controversial former Kentucky player alive. Bret Bearup knows this. Not so long ago, he didn't mind the attention. Times change.

In the good old days of the late 1990s, Bearup was the man behind the college basketball curtain. Whether he was or was not steering high school recruits to certain friends in the college coaching business—and for the record, Bearup says he was not—that was the perception.

Whether he was or was not steering high school players and college underclassmen into the NBA draft—and again Bearup says he was not—that, too, was the perception.

For a while, the attention was flattering.

"You know, the perception that I had all this power wasn't totally unwelcome to me," Bearup says. "But after a while, people start writing things or saying things that just aren't true. People that really don't know what's going on act like they do know, and I've just gotten tired of that whole thing."

All the attention certainly hasn't hurt Bearup's business. Ten years after leaving a flourishing career as an attorney, he has turned his original one-man business, ProTrust Capital, into the No. 1 money management firm of NBA players. In late 2004 Bearup said he represented 75 or 80 NBA players, roughly 20 percent of the NBA's active roster, including stars Kevin Garnett and Tim Duncan. Bearup also represented close to 100 Major League Baseball and NFL players, as well as entertainers like Alanis Morissette and Hootie and the Blowfish.

Between meeting with current clients and courting new ones, Bearup estimated that he spends nearly half of the year on the road. The other half,

88

BRET BEARUP

Years lettered: 1980-81, 1982-83, 1983-84, 1984-85
Career totals: 410 points, 308 rebounds, 72 assists, 20 blocks

though, he spends at home in the Atlanta area, working from an office in his house and doting on his wife and three children.

"When I'm in town," he says, "I'm at home."

But there have been tradeoffs, most notably to his reputation. Don't get the wrong idea: Bret Bearup is widely respected among NBA players and front-office types, and do not be at all surprised if he ends up one day working in an NBA franchise's front office. He is respected by college coaches, and he is adored by college and high school players who envision making a fortune in professional basketball and entrust Bearup to make their fortunes even bigger.

Still, rumors fly. Innuendo swirls. And at times Bearup has had to pay the price in the form of friendships lost, or at least weakened. That's definitely the case with Florida coach Billy Donovan, an assistant coach at Kentucky from 1990-94. In the late 1990s Bearup and Donovan were tight, and while they remain friends, their friendship has changed. It has had to.

Eddie Fogler saw to that.

Fogler was the coach at South Carolina in 1998 when he launched his infamous attack on Donovan and Bearup, claiming Bearup was funneling players to Donovan. Fogler's primary concern was a European tour Bearup had been conducting each summer for the country's top high school players. Many of those players, Fogler noted, ended up playing for Bearup's good friend at Florida.

"Want to hear the new gig? This is a beauty," Fogler said at the Southeastern Conference's 1998 Media Days. "The new gig—it's legal. Now, is it ethical? You be the judge. The new gig is financial managers, money managers, who put together summer trips."

Donovan, whose program has never been found guilty of recruiting violations—even when the NCAA investigated Florida in the late 1990s—fired back at Fogler.

"I resent the things Eddie Fogler said," Donovan said. "For him to attack my integrity and the integrity of anyone from Florida shows he doesn't have enough class, enough courage to come right out and confront me about it. ... It shows absolutely no guts on his part."

Bearup told *The State* newspaper in Columbia, S.C., that Fogler's attack was off target.

"I'm stunned and saddened that Eddie thinks I'm in cahoots with some college coach," Bearup said. "Eddie needs to get his facts straight. College coaches are kind of paranoid to begin with. If they get beat on a recruit, all too often you hear a third party is responsible for it."

Eventually, though, Bearup stopped putting on his European tours. They were essentially a chance for him to develop relationships with the country's best amateur players, knowing full well that many of them would reach the NBA and need a money manager once they got there. The trips were legal, according to the NCAA, but Bearup ultimately decided they weren't worth the hassle.

His friendship with Donovan, too, has been cut back.

"My relationship with Billy Donovan has never been the same because of that," Bearup says. "It painted him in a negative light, and this is one guy who follows the rules more than anyone I know. We used to be better friends than we are. We're still friends, but I wish it was different. When we get together Billy can feel the eyes, and I can feel the eyes. We sit down and talk, and people think we're scheming to get a big-time recruit to Florida."

A quarter-century earlier, Bearup was a big-time recruit himself. A six-foot-nine forward out of Greenlawn, N.Y., he was a McDonald's All-American when he signed to play for Kentucky in 1980. He never became a star for the Wildcats, and even opted to redshirt what would have been his sophomore season in 1981-82 rather than waste the year behind Melvin Turpin, Charles Hurt and Chuck Verderber. But by his senior season, Bearup had become a solid player for the Wildcats, averaging 6.3 points and 5.6 rebounds in the first season after the departure of twin towers Turpin and Sam Bowie.

Bearup played briefly in Europe before returning to Kentucky's law school in 1986, graduating in 1989. He spent four years with the powerful Louisville law firm of Greenbaum, Doll & McDonald, where he handled arbitration for the firm's securities clients.

"Generally I was defending brokers like Smith Barney or Merrill Lynch against claims from investors," Bearup says. "To defend claims about unsuitable investments, you'd really have to know what a suitable investment is. I did a lot of research to try to make myself an expert as soon as possible."

As it turns out, Bearup didn't love practicing law as much as he loved making investments. He left Greenbaum, Doll in 1993 for Hilliard Lyons, a 150-year-old investment firm with branches all over the country. After a year there, Bearup branched out on his own and formed ProTrust.

Bearup knew athletes needed help with their investments. Who better to help them than a money manager who once had been in their shoes—a big-time recruit, then a player in a big-time college program, and finally a professional athlete?

"I just took a look at players who were either working with somebody else or not working with anybody," Bearup says, "and I said, 'Why not me?'"

At first, his name recognition as an ex-Wildcat helped get his business off the ground. After that, though, it's all about the money. And Bearup knows money. He'd better—in the summer of 2004, his NBA clients alone signed contracts worth more than $300 million.

By that summer, Bearup felt his firm had grown big enough. For the first time he didn't spend the summer at the various recruiting camps run by Nike, Reebok or Adidas. He didn't need to court any more clients—he had plenty.

Some of his clients were more notorious than others. Two years after the Fogler flap, Bearup's name again surfaced in an ugly light when a New York newspaper reported that he had given St. John's guard Erick Barkley $50,000 to join his firm. That would have been a major breach of NCAA rules, not to mention ethics, but the newspaper story was wrong. Bearup had arranged a $50,000 line of credit for Barkley, yes, but it came after the season—after the player had decided to turn pro.

Big difference.

Still, Bearup was an easy target. That same spring, with Florida threatening to win the Southeastern Conference championship, Fogler was at it again. He said the league's MVP would have to be Bearup. In 1998 Fogler had taken it upon himself to speak for former Kentucky coach Rick Pitino, saying Pitino had called Bearup "a disgrace to Kentucky basketball."

For his part, Bearup acknowledged that he had felt unwelcome at Kentucky when Pitino was coach, but said that changed when Tubby Smith took over in 1997. When Kentucky's 1984 Final Four team had its 20th reunion in 2004, Bearup was there.

"I have a good relationship with Tubby," Bearup says. "I just have to be really careful with regard to the recruiting stuff. Kentucky's really the only school that can get in trouble because of what I do. As an alum, I'm a 'representative of the institution' [according to the NCAA]. By keeping my distance I've lost some [Kentucky] guys that could have been clients, but that's okay. I don't want to get my alma mater in trouble. There are plenty of players out there."

Where Have You Gone?

CAMERON MILLS

By the time he was 12 years old, Cameron Mills had the rest of his life pretty much figured out. He wanted to play college basketball for Kentucky, and then he wanted to go into the ministry.

Looking back on it now, you might figure Mills had it easy. He did play basketball for the Wildcats, even becoming a folk hero for his role on the 1997 and '98 teams that played for national championships. And after that he did go into the ministry, where to this day he remains a nationally pursued public speaker.

Fairy tale stuff. End of story, right?

Not quite.

For starters, Mills almost attended Georgia. As for what happened after college, well, Mills never planned on getting divorced, he never planned to take a year sabbatical from his ministry, and he definitely didn't plan to work as a bank teller.

"It hasn't always been easy," he says. "The Bible doesn't say it's always going to be easy."

The rest of the story starts in 1994 with Mills, an all-state senior guard at Dunbar High in Lexington, desperately wanting to play for Kentucky but going virtually unrecruited by Rick Pitino's staff. Mills had a variety of scholarship offers and had all but decided to sign with Georgia. However, he wanted to make one last attempt to play for Pitino, whose summer basketball camps he had been attending for years.

On the morning of national signing day, Mills held off signing with Georgia while his father went to the Kentucky basketball offices to explain the situation. His father is Terry Mills, who had played for Adolph Rupp at

CAMERON MILLS

Years lettered: 1994-95, 1995-96, 1997-98, 1998-99
Career totals: 365 points, 98 rebounds, 53 assists,
81 three-pointers

Kentucky from 1969-71, and Terry Mills's plan was to speak with longtime Kentucky equipment manager Bill Keightley. Visiting the equipment manager might sound like a strange way to decipher the coaching staff's plans, but Keightley has never been just an equipment manager. He's had his finger on the pulse of Kentucky basketball since the 1960s, was nicknamed "Mr. Wildcat," and in 1997 had a jersey retired in his honor. So, the elder Mills went to visit Keightley in early 1994, and when he got there he found a bonus: Assistant coach Billy Donovan was in the room, too.

Terry Mills laid out the situation for both of them. Cameron explains it like so:

"Dad said, 'Here's the deal: Georgia's about to sign Cameron, but he really wants to play here. Would you all be interested?' Billy [Donovan] just says, 'No, we're set at the two-guard spot.' But somebody—and this is where the story gets fuzzy—suggested walking on.

"Billy said something like, 'Tell Cameron if he wants to walk on, we'll take him. He won't have to try out—he'll be on the team.' Coach Pitino had seen me play at his basketball camps, so I guess he knew I would be good enough to have around in practice.

"Well, Dad left their offices and came right over to the high school, to Dunbar. He got there at 11 a.m., got me out of class and brought me to the office. He said, 'Okay, they want you to walk on.' All I heard was, 'They want you.' I asked Dad if we could afford it, and he said yes. So I never signed with Georgia."

Kentucky has the 1998 national championship banner to prove it.

That Kentucky team had six future NBA players as well as Allen Edwards and Heshimu Evans, but it was Mills who hit two of the biggest shots of the season. Both were three-pointers, and both came in the final eight minutes of the 1998 title game to rally the Wildcats past Utah.

Mills had done the same thing the year before, when he was 17 for 27 on three-pointers (63 percent) in that NCAA tournament. Kentucky's loss in the 1997 title game to Arizona didn't obscure the contribution of the former walk-on. "We could not have reached the Final Four," Pitino would say, "without Cameron Mills."

Mills ended his career as Kentucky's all-time leader in three-point accuracy, hitting 47.4 percent from 1995-98. That kind of marksmanship attracted the attention of professional teams overseas, but Mills told the prospective agents who called that he didn't want to look into it.

"I never pursued it," Mills says. "I felt I'd been called to the ministry."

Mills began heading in that direction even at Dunbar High, where he was president of the school's chapter of the Fellowship of Christian Athletes. Mills joined the University of Kentucky chapter of FCA as a college freshman, and soon was touring the state to visit schools and church groups. He remembers the first time state FCA director Max Appel asked him to speak, and the profound effect that speaking engagement had on his eventual career path.

"One weekend I went in the [FCA] van to Maysville, Kentucky, and Max looked back at me and asked me if I'd like to speak this time," Mills says. "Well, sure. On the way up there, about an hour drive, I got a napkin and put some thoughts together on sexual purity. Afterward, I had a number of kids come up and thank me for what I said, and one was a little girl, crying her eyes out. She looked at me and said, 'I wish I'd heard this two weeks ago.' At that moment I knew.

"When I was 12, I felt I was called to ministry—maybe a youth minister, but I wasn't sure what. Then all of a sudden this happened, and I said, 'Maybe this is it. If I can have this kind of impact in one moment, then this is what I need to be doing.' I was so encouraged by that moment that every time Max asked me to go, I went."

Word spread. By the time Mills graduated from Kentucky in the spring of 1998, his secretary—who also happened to be his mother—had almost 18 months of speaking engagements lined up for him to do.

His first speaking engagement was in early June 1998, before an audience of close to 1,500 at a church in Middlesboro, Kentucky. The next day he spoke to about 40 people in Louisville.

"I spoke to nursing homes, churches, big groups, small ones," Mills says. "It just varied."

Before 1998 was out, Mills found himself at a ministry conference in Arizona, where he met his future wife. She accompanied Cameron on his ministry, sometimes speaking to groups herself, but the marriage didn't last. An old ankle injury from her college days led to surgery shortly into the marriage, and the ankle kept her in constant pain. Her quest for relief took her to some of the country's most well-known medical facilities—Johns Hopkins, the Mayo Clinic—but the pain cast a pall over the entire marriage, and by 2001 she had returned to Arizona, alone. The divorce was final in October 2003.

During the separation Mills began finding it difficult to muster enthusiasm for his speaking engagements.

"I'd been feeling that I was stagnating," he says. "I'd never been to seminary and I'd been feeling like I needed more Bible—I still do—but with the separation, I just felt I was preaching out of an empty instead of out of an overflow. After she left, it was a struggle sometimes to get into the car and drive where I was supposed to speak and to speak. That's not what ministry is supposed to be. There are times in anything where you can get burned out, but in my mind I wasn't speaking enough to be getting burned out. I felt like I needed to take a year off and learn—a sabbatical year to soak up instead of pour out."

Mills went to Denton, Texas, to participate in Tommy Nelson's discipleship program at Denton Bible Church. The nine-month program was built around Bible classes early in the morning, but during the day students were expected to get a job—at least the students like Mills, who needed income to pay for rent, food and the like. Mills found work through the Dallas chapter of the Kentucky Alumni Association, and began his job as a bank teller.

That turned out okay, except for the bad check he cashed for $1,200.

"It was a very well done, fraudulent check," Mills says. "That was scary, but they understood. For the most part I was a better teller than I would have thought. I'd been in school or in the ministry, so I'd never had a nine-to-five kind of job. I was excited about the program, the job, the whole thing."

Invigorated after the year in Denton, Mills returned to Lexington in 2003 ready to resume his ministry. He remains in demand through his non-profit organization, Cameron Mills Ministries, and through the Premiere Speakers Bureau, which has a stable of Christian speakers, including Pat Boone, Bobby Bowden and Oliver North.

Mills also has created the "Filthy Rags" clothing line—T-shirts and hats, mainly—which he named after a line in Isaiah 64:6, and runs a series of basketball camps throughout the state. The camps are equal doses of basketball and ministry. That's who Cameron Mills is. It's who he's always been.

"I was always real open about my faith, and as a Kentucky player there's a lot of face time—newspapers, television, local and national," Mills says. "It wasn't a mission or anything to share my faith, it was just who I am. It just comes out in my life."

Where Have You Gone?

JOE B. HALL

Joe B. Hall remembers the first weekend of the rest of his life, in the fall of 1985, after he had retired from coaching following the 1984 season. It's a fond memory now, almost two decades after his last game on the Kentucky sideline, but at the time Hall felt empty, almost confused, like a deep-sea diver whose body had grown accustomed to the pressure of the ocean. Divers who come up for air too quickly get decompression sickness, called the bends.

That was Hall in the fall of 1985, undergoing decompression sickness in his first basketball season in decades without a basketball team. He was flummoxed by this vague new concept called "free time."

"My first weekend off, and I didn't have any plans," he said recently from his condominium in Lexington. "I was kind of lost. I kind of wandered around home thinking about what I should be doing."

Answer: Nothing.

As you can imagine, Hall soon found the pleasure in such nothingness. That pleasure continues today, with Hall filling in the holes in his schedule not with recruiting calls or speaking engagements, but with his grandchildren or his wife or time spent in the outdoors.

In 1985, though, it was a difficult transition from Joe B. Hall, Kentucky basketball coach, to Joe B. Hall, vice president of Central Bank in Lexington. This was a man who had given the previous 30 years of his life to other people's children, and here it was, the start of another college basketball season, and the only children demanding his time were his own.

Wait a minute, Joe B. Hall remembers saying to himself. This might be the start of something pretty good.

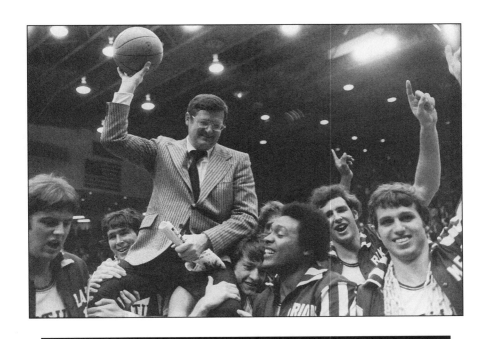

JOE B. HALL

Head coach: 1973-85
Honors: 1978 national coach of the year;
retired jersey (no number)
Career totals: 297-100; 1978 NCAA championship

"It was a revelation," he says. "Imagine, realizing you have time to yourself, with no hangover responsibilities. That was a good feeling."

Life was good for Hall at Kentucky, where he led the Wildcats to the 1978 national championship and won 297 games in 13 years before leaving on his terms—and leaving his replacement, Eddie Sutton, enough talent to go 32-4 in 1986. But life has been good for Hall in the 20 years since, too. Life has been so good that he has succumbed to the siren call of coaching just once.

That's right. Joe B. Hall's resignation from Kentucky wasn't his resignation from coaching. He spent one more season on the sideline, and if you didn't know about it, don't feel bad. It happened on the other side of the world, where Hall spent the 1996 season coaching a team in a Japanese league.

A Japanese women's league.

The team played one game a week for ten weeks, and won six of them. The year before, Hall says, that same team had played 20 games and won just twice.

"I had a lot of fun over there," Hall says.

Well, why not? There was no recruiting involved in the job, because this was professional basketball. There were no speaking engagements—no one in Japan could understand Hall's Kentucky twang—and very few media engagements thanks to a lack of interest in women's professional basketball in Japan. You know what this was? This was coaching at its purest, and Hall always did love to coach. Truth be told, he liked the other stuff, too—the recruiting, the speaking, the media. But he just would have liked a little less of the other stuff.

"I didn't mind any of it," he says. "I especially enjoyed watching high schools play, but the only thing at Kentucky was there were extreme demands on your time. Compare coaching at Ole Miss to coaching at Kentucky. It's night and day. I probably had five speaking requests every day, and there were some you just felt you couldn't turn down."

Hall turned down a horde of schools after resigning from Kentucky. Southern Cal wanted him to help the Trojans mount a challenge to UCLA. South Florida was just starting to build its program and wanted Hall to lead the way. Other schools—many others—called because after all, at all stops Hall's lifetime winning percentage was 373-156. The schools continued to call even though Hall rejected overture after overture, including a chance in 1969 to coach St. Louis, which he accepted for a week before changing his mind and coming back home. In his mind, he was a Kentucky guy: Raised outside of Lexington in Cynthiana, a card-carrying member of the Blue Mist. Then, he was a Kentucky student and player, then a Kentucky graduate, then Kentucky legend Adolph Rupp's assistant, then Rupp's replacement.

"I'm a Kentuckian, and there's no place else for me to go," he says. "I would not have considered coaching at another school."

Still, schools kept calling. After all, Hall was only 56. He wasn't exactly an old coach.

Hall said no to all of them, because Hall wanted to keep it that way. He never wanted to become an old coach. He had seen what that had done to his mentor, Rupp, who had resigned under pressure after the 1972 season at age 70. Rupp's record had declined as his age had increased, and Hall saw a correlation.

"Coach Rupp was not in good health, and I thought he stayed too long," Hall says. "He was 70 when he retired. I just felt like you needed to be closer to the generation of players you were recruiting and coaching to have a good relationship. Get out before you lost that ability to communicate with your players.

"I was at the age of 55 or 56, so I could get out of coaching and still be useful in some other business and I really enjoyed banking. That was a great experience to finally realize what 'Thank God it's Friday' meant."

For Hall, down time meant wading in a creek or pond near his house, or hanging out in a goose blind in western Kentucky. Even after turning 75, Hall loves the outdoors like a little boy, his passion taking him all over the world on his own dime: fishing trips from Alaska to Zambia, Canada to Costa Rica, Belize to Brazil and back again. Hall still gets recognized, of course. Kentucky Nation never forgets a hero, even when he's walking down the street in Palma Majorca or ice fishing in Alaska.

"Happens all the time," he says.

Even now, Hall will wax poetic about the pursuit of the peacock bass, which he has battled in Amazon tributaries in Brazil.

"That's the greatest fishing anyone could ever do," he says. "I've caught hundreds but never had one mounted. They're just topwater-hitting sport fish, a beautiful fish. Their coloration is the reason for their name. [They] get up to 30 pounds, and there's fighting. It's just the Mecca of fishing."

Mecca of fishing, Mecca of college basketball—yeah, Joe B. Hall has lived a pretty good life. He's still living it, too, including a recent radio venture with former Louisville coach Denny Crum that began in March 2004 on airwaves around the state. *The Joe B. and Denny Show* airs two hours a day, five days a week. They talk life and basketball, which in Kentucky is the same thing. At noon it's time to go, and Hall brings his waders to work.

There's nothing but time, and there's a pond right down the road.

Where Have You Gone?

LARRY STEELE

Larry Steele was an All-SEC guard at Kentucky, where he played along-side all-time Kentucky scoring leader Dan Issel in 1969 and '70 and then Tom Payne in '71, when Payne crossed Kentucky basketball's color line. In the pros Steele won an NBA championship in 1977 with the Trail Blazers, who retired his No. 15 jersey. He later spent seven years coaching a college team in Portland.

Then he got out of basketball and became really interesting.

Okay, fine. Steele was interesting when he was involved exclusively with basketball. At Kentucky he was a three-year starter from 1969-71. With Steele scoring from the perimeter, distracting defenses just enough for Issel and then Payne to become superstars, the Wildcats went 71-13 in those three seasons.

At Portland, Steele started for the city's first and still only NBA champi-onship team in a fascinating lineup that included hippie big man Bill Walton at center, enforcer Maurice Lucas at power forward and future NBA executive Dave Twardzik at point guard. On an individual level that 1976-77 season was the zenith of Steele's career as well, because that was the sea-son he averaged a career-best 10.3 points per game.

Then he coached the University of Portland from 1987-94 and yadda yadda yadda.

Look, do you want to know what makes the guy interesting or not?

Not even Steele knows what makes him interesting, which makes him even more interesting. For example, after nearly an hour on the phone, just as he's about to hang up, Steele mentions something about heading back to

LARRY STEELE

Years lettered: 1968-69, 1969-70, 1971-72, 1973-74
Honors: All-SEC 1970-71
Career totals: 781 points, 499 rebounds, 216 assists

his house on the river. Most people, when they say they live on the river, they're talking about a house or a condo overlooking some water.

Not Steele. He lives on the river. His house floats.

More on that in a minute, but there's other interesting stuff to get to first. For example, Steele is a vegetarian. That doesn't exactly make him unique in the 21st century United States, but it probably does make him unique among ex-Kentucky basketball stars. If there's another former All-SEC pick in Kentucky basketball lore who has sworn off meat to live on a diet of breads, fruits and vegetables, let him speak up now.

Silence. Told you: Steele's a different kind of a guy.

And then there's his Kentucky basketball tickets. Steele has been a season ticket holder since 1972, holding two tickets to every game at Rupp Arena. That's a lot of history for one man to see: Goose Givens to Sam Bowie to Kenny Walker. And then Rex Chapman to Jamal Mashburn to Tayshaun Prince. Of all that history spread over more than three decades, Steele has seen exactly zero games.

None.

"I don't even know where my seats are," he says. "Since I'm an alum, my seats move down [closer to the court] every year, so I bet they're pretty good. But I've never been."

The seats don't go empty. Though he hasn't lived in Kentucky since he graduated from the university in 1971, Steele still has plenty of friends around Lexington. That's who gets the tickets.

It's hard to get to a Kentucky game from Portland, which is where Steele has lived for most of the past 30-plus years, but even if he lived in Lexington he might not have time to attend all the home games. Or even very many.

Steele has kept busy since "retiring" as the University of Portland's coach in 1994. He hasn't worked for anyone since, but that doesn't mean Steele hasn't worked. Basketball may have been his calling, but it wasn't his only one.

"I guess I've got the spirit of an entrepreneur," he says.

He guesses? As of late 2004, Steele had his hand in about ten different business ventures. Some ventures were related, like his various consulting enterprises that seem intertwined or his basketball camp and conference center that are held at the same resort in Vernonia, Oregon. Some ventures are unique unto themselves, like his marketing company that uses emerging technology or his flooring company that has a patent for a new kind of basketball court.

That's right. Larry Steele is trying to build a better basketball court.

"We're talking about basketball courts for the private sector—for health clubs, places like that," says Steele, who is working with a local engineer on the floor's design. "We think this is the perfect floor. It's exactly like any other floor in terms of quality, but it comes in four foot-by-20 foot sections instead of board by board. You walk into the gym and it looks like a continuous floor, but on this one, you can take it up if you need to expand or change [the business], and it's a lot cheaper to install."

Steele goes on to explain the tax benefits of his proposed court—it has something to do with depreciation—but the explanation is too difficult for a basketball writer to comprehend.

In a lot of ways, everything about Steele's business acumen is difficult to comprehend. This guy went from a basketball lifer to a diversified businessman with interests ranging from health food restaurants (he's talking with one of Portland's premier chefs about a new eatery) to day spas (he's chairman of Aequis Spas in Portland) to advising companies on corporate development (through his consulting firm, Integris).

Ask Steele how he made such a transition, and he does something outlandish. He compares basketball to business.

"It's very simple," he says. "Most basketball people, if they really stop and think about it, they love basketball, but it's not the basketball that keeps them intrigued. It's the competitive nature of what they do. Basketball is a vehicle for a lot of competitive people to express themselves. In business, it's just as competitive as a sport. You're just directing your competitive nature toward other areas. It's actually a very easy switch. I miss some of the basketball, but it's taken care of in my life by doing some camps."

Ah, yes. The camps. Around Portland he's still best known for that 1977 title season, which does wonders for his annual Larry Steele Basketball Camp, which is nearing its 20th year and has seen close to 20,000 kids pass through. Steele holds three or four weekly camps each summer at the Cedar Ridge Retreat & Conference Center, which stays busy the rest of the year by hosting business groups.

The basketball camp and conference center provide Steele with the financial foundation for everything else he does, allowing him to dabble in all kinds of start-up enterprises. And Steele loves to dabble, even knowing the failure rate is high. He says a successful entrepreneur gets "off the ground" with one out of every six or seven ideas. His most painful failure happened in the early 1990s, when he opened a movie rental store. That was a good idea—such a good idea that Hollywood Video opened a franchise down the street, putting Steele's store out of business.

"These entrepreneurial tendencies I have, they don't all pan out," he says. "Putting together businesses is getting people together. It takes a competitive nature to put together companies that will compete with others, and I've always had a competitive nature."

Of all his ventures, Steele is most optimistic about the basketball court. It could be the next big thing. Or this sentence might be the last you hear of it.

Either way, buoyed by his camp and retreat center, Steele will sleep soundly on his floating home on the Willamette River near downtown Portland. He and Britt Bensen, a woman he calls his "business and life partner," are among 38 homeowners at the moorage.

"We look right down the river into the city," Steele says. "Incredibly, we live almost in downtown Portland, and we have geese, raccoons, purple martins, ducks. Every weekend we have 300 geese in the water in front of our house. It's one of the most unique places to live anywhere."

There's only one problem with the neighborhood: the name. Steele's community is called The Oregon Yacht Club, which is slightly misleading (these are homes, not yachts) and definitely pretentious. "It sounds snobby," Steele says.

Steele could try to lobby the other homeowners to change the name, but he has enough on his plate. Probably he has too much on his plate, what with his camp and retreat center and consulting. And his basketball court, day spa, restaurant ...

"I'm not really proud of the fact that I'm too busy," he says. "It's not like I'm happy with that. I'm trying to reduce the time I spend on these things."

Too busy? Reduce his entrepreneurial instincts?

Interesting. Very interesting.

Where Have You Gone?

GIMEL MARTINEZ

Gimel Martinez is alive and well and teaching low-post moves in Dublin, Ohio.

"I do know how to play in the post," Martinez says. "I had some very good teachers back then. I retained it, but maybe I didn't put everything they taught me to use."

Maybe not. Martinez played for the Wildcats in the early 1990s, the era of "Pitino's Bombinos" in which Kentucky chucked three-pointers from every position. That included Martinez, a six-foot-eight power forward or center who was constantly loitering around the three-point arc, hunting his shot. He found it 115 times in his career, including 97 times in his final two seasons. If that was more three-pointers than Kentucky fans ever dreamed a big man like Martinez would shoot, well, they weren't alone.

It was more three-pointers than Martinez ever dreamed he'd shoot, too.

As a high school senior in Miami, Martinez was an all-state player who did whatever he wanted on the court—as long as it was inside the three-point arc. He remembers taking two three-pointers his entire career, with both coming in his final game, the state championship of his senior season.

"I made 50 percent," he says mischievously, knowing that figure sounds more impressive than saying, "I made one."

The crowd included then-Kentucky coach Rick Pitino and a UK assistant, Herb Sendek. Martinez says he shot those three-pointers for their benefit.

"I was trying to get warmed up for the Bombinos," he says.

Martinez scored 719 points in four seasons at Kentucky, helping the Wildcats in their transition from 14-14 in Pitino's debut in 1989-90 to the

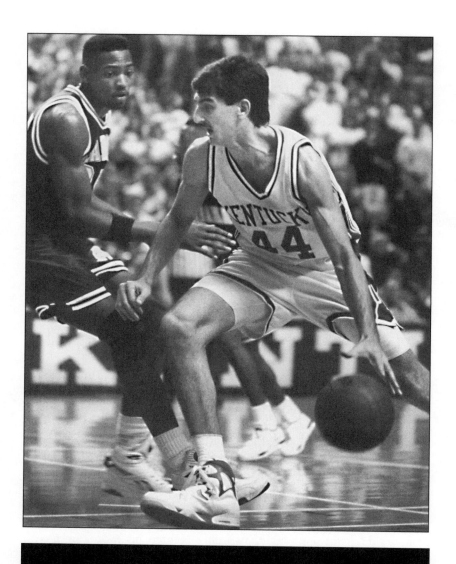

GIMEL MARTINEZ

Years lettered: 1990-91, 1991-92, 1992-93, 1993-94
Career totals: 719 points, 338 rebounds, 137 assists, 58 blocks

powerhouse that won the 1996 national championship. After college, Martinez took his unorthodox skill set—big man's body, small man's shot—to Japan for three seasons of professional basketball there, followed by a year each at Puerto Rico and France. Although he was the son of Cuban immigrants, Martinez counted as an American on the roster of international teams, most of which allow a maximum of two Americans per team. That meant Martinez was competing not for one of 12 roster spots every year overseas, but for one of two spots. However, that's not why his professional career ended after five years at the age of 27.

"I started having kids," he says. "It was time to settle down."

Indeed, Martinez had met his wife while they were at the University of Kentucky. Amid Martinez's routine of seven months overseas, five months in America, Gimel and Missy were married and had their first child, also named Gimel, while Martinez was playing in France. After that season was completed in 1999, he returned to the States for good. He and Missy put down roots in Dublin, near her family in Columbus, Ohio, and Martinez took classes at Ohio Dominican College.

Martinez's plan was twofold: One, get his bachelor's degree; Two, get into college coaching.

A funny thing happened on the way to college coaching. ...

Martinez took a job instead with his wife's family. For four generations his in-laws had run a company that sells rigging equipment for overhead lifting—stuff like bridge, gantry, monorail, fixed hoists and jib wall mounts.

No, Martinez didn't know a wall mount from Rick Mount, but at the time he was taking classes at Ohio Dominican and also helping to support his wife and child, with another child (Myles) on the way. His wife's family offered a part-time job in sales at their company, and Martinez took it, discovering that juggling work and school wasn't as difficult as juggling basketball and school had been a decade earlier at Kentucky.

Martinez's plan, now, was threefold: One, get his bachelor's degree; Two, save money by working for the family business; Three, get into college coaching.

Two out of three ain't bad, right? Martinez graduated from Ohio Dominican, fulfilling a lifelong goal, and then moved on to full-time work with his in-laws. That's a good thing. No, really—it has been a good thing.

"Not too many people can say they've got a relationship with their in-laws the way I do," Martinez says. "I feel very fortunate because we obviously see each other all the time, and they're great people."

Along the way, Martinez has had offers to get into coaching. They've been from small colleges and high schools in the Columbus area, offers to serve as an assistant, but Martinez has turned all of them down. He's willing to listen to offers to assist a Division I program, but for now he has a good thing going with the family business, and with a wife and two small kids ... well, starting as an assistant coach in high school probably wouldn't be fair to his family.

Coaching on a part-time basis also has been an option—but that probably wouldn't be fair to the team.

"With my job I travel quite a bit, so I can't commit to something like that," Martinez says. "I still would like to coach. The door's not shut—you never can have any locked doors."

Martinez still gets his basketball fix as a player and as a coach. As a player he's a familiar sight in area leagues—tall and dark, with an unusually thick head of hair and an equally unusual penchant for hitting three-pointers. The only difference between the Martinez terrorizing the adults in Ohio and the one who played for Kentucky is the facial hair. Back then, he wore a mustache. Today he goes for the goatee. Inquiring minds want to know, correct?

As a coach, Martinez works with his two sons and also at a variety of local camps and clinics he helps conduct. Most camps are broken down into positions, and the 6-8 Martinez handles the post players. To ensure that his large pupils don't get any ideas about floating out to the perimeter, Martinez doesn't tell them about his days as Pitino's biggest Bombino.

"I keep that part quiet," he says. "From me, all they get is work on the low post."

A funny thing, life.

"I'm satisfied," he says.

REST IN PEACE:
DECEASED WILDCATS

Some legends of Kentucky basketball were easier to find than others. They were written about one final time, in a section of the newspaper called the obituaries.

However, this is not a chapter of mourning, but one of celebration. For the Kentucky basketball program produced some of the state's leaders in commerce and philanthropy, medicine and dentistry. Not to mention an internationally recognized breeder of sheep.

They are dead but they are not forgotten; their accomplishments in life reached far beyond their ability to play a little basketball.

ERMAL ALLEN

Years lettered: 1939-40, 1940-41, 1941-42
Honors: All-SEC 1941-42

If Wallace "Wah Wah" Jones wasn't the most well-rounded athlete ever to compete for the University of Kentucky, Allen was. He played four sports in college—football, basketball, golf and track—and was talented enough to have been an All-SEC forward and a three-year starter at tailback, while the UK golf team lost just one match in his three seasons. Although Allen won the Kentucky Amateur twice and won the Tri-State title three times, his future was football. He spent 13 seasons with the Dallas Cowboys, breaking new ground in scouting in the 1970s as Tom Landry's director of research and development. He retired in 1983 and died five years later at age 69. Among the mourners at his Lexington funeral were Gov. John Y. Brown.

CLIFF BARKER

Years lettered: 1946-47, 1947-48, 1948-49
Honors: Retired jersey No. 22

A prisoner of war after being shot down in Germany during World War II, Barker eventually resumed his Kentucky career in 1946-47 with exceptional ballhandling skills. As it turns out, after being shot out of the sky in his B-17 bomber, Barker had spent his 16 months in captivity bouncing and passing a volleyball. In 1949 he celebrated his final game at home with a 65-footer at the buzzer in Kentucky's 70-37 win against Vanderbilt. Barker coached and played in the NBA, but spent the bulk of his adult life coaching basketball at high schools in Indiana, Kentucky and Florida. He died in 1998 at age 77.

HENRY BESUDEN

Years lettered: 1925-26

A family emergency ended Besuden's playing days but ignited his prominent career as a farmer. It was 1926, and as Besuden was preparing to leave for a Kentucky basketball road trip, he was served a lien on the family farm by federal marshals. Told the farm would be sold to pay back taxes unless other arrangements could be made, Besuden withdrew from school and rescued the farm. He later became famous for breeding Southdown sheep, winning a record 12 grand championships at the International Livestock Exposition in Chicago from 1950-71. Before his death in 1985 at age 81, Besuden received a telegram from President Reagan that applauded his work in agriculture. "Your accomplishments in this field have improved the economic climate of your state," Reagan's note read, "and strengthened the farming system of your fellow citizens."

LARRY BOECK

Honors: Member, U.S. Basketball Writers Association Hall of Fame

He didn't play for the Wildcats, but Boeck played a huge role in Kentucky history nonetheless. He was the Louisville sports writer who broke the story for the *Courier-Journal* that three stars from Kentucky's 1954 team were graduate students and therefore ineligible for the NCAA Tournament. That story reportedly led to a near-fight between Boeck and Kentucky assistant Harry Lancaster. The Wildcats chose not to compete in the tournament, costing them a shot at another national championship—not to mention what would have been their only undefeated champion. Boeck, a hall of fame member of the U.S. Basketball Writers Association, left sports writing in 1966 to work for the University of Louisville, where he was employed in 1972 when he died at age 52.

RALPH CARLISLE

Years lettered: 1934-35, 1935-36, 1936-37
Honors: All-SEC 1935-36, 1936-37

Jackson-Carlisle Gym at Lexington basketball powerhouse Lafayette High is half-named for the ex-Wildcat who led Lafayette to 11 district, six regional and three Sweet 16 championships from 1945-61, with a state title in 1953. Carlisle, an All-SEC forward in 1936 and '37, won nearly 500 games as the coach at three Kentucky high schools: Lafayette, Kavanaugh and Madison. He died in 1999 at age 84.

MAURICE JACKSON

Years lettered: 1932-33

The namesake of the other half of the Carlisle-Jackson Gym at Lafayette High, Jackson became the Generals' first coach when the Lexington school opened in 1939—six years after Jackson had played on Rupp's first team at Kentucky. In 1942, Jackson led Lafayette High to the first state championship by a Lexington school in nearly two decades. Jackson's coaching career ended when he joined the U.S. Army during World War II. He became a captain, then worked as a training officer with disabled veterans. He later spent 12 years as a sheriff's deputy, then successfully ran for Fayette County sheriff in 1969. He died in 1995 at age 84.

DAN CHANDLER

Years lettered: 1952-53, 1953-54, 1954-55

This member of Kentucky's 1953 national championship team has an intricate claim to fame. First there's his father, former Kentucky governor and Major League Baseball commissioner Happy Chandler. Second, Dan Chandler was involved in one of the most famous on-court fights in school history, a pregame brawl in 1955 with Alabama's Jim Bogan, who was eight inches taller than the five-foot-11 Chandler. According to sports writers in attendance, Chandler held his own. An undisputed tough guy, he later became a casino executive in Las Vegas. Chandler died in 2004 at age 70.

HENRY DENHAM

Years lettered: 1938-39
Honors: All-SEC 1935-36, 1936-37

Better known as a football player, Denham played three seasons for Kentucky basketball coach Adolph Rupp and was ultimately inducted into the College Football Hall of Fame. His best work, though, would come later. Denham became a general practitioner and surgeon, spending two years with the U.S. Army Medical Corps in Vienna during the post-World War II reconstruction of Europe before returning to his hometown of Maysville, Kentucky. It was there in 1956 that he co-founded the Denham Medical Clinic. He died in 2001 at age 83.

RUSSELL "DUKE" ELLINGTON

Years lettered: 1934-35, 1935-36

Ellington turned heads in the 1930s with his transfer from Louisville to Kentucky, where he played basketball and football. He eventually opened an antique business in Lexington named the Ellington House before dying in 1986 at age 73.

WALTER HATCHER

Years lettered: 1936-37

This part-time player in the 1930s was a full-fledged hero in World War II, serving in the Battle of the Bulge and receiving a Bronze Star. He was a dentist for 43 years who dabbled in banking and the coal business in

Pikeville, Kentucky, accumulating enough wealth to donate the land that became the Pike County Airport. There, Hatcher Field bears his name. He died in 1994 at age 78.

BASIL HAYDEN

Years lettered: 1919-20, 1920-21, 1921-22
Honors: All-American, 1920-21; retired jersey (no number)

He was Kentucky's first basketball All-American and the oldest ex-Wildcat until his death in 2003 at age 103. Hayden also is among the only coaches in Kentucky history to post a losing record. That happened in 1926-27, when the Wildcats were 3-13—their last losing record until 1988-89. Hayden did much better in business, working as a banker, accountant and hospital administrator.

ELLIS JOHNSON

Years lettered: 1930-31, 1931-32, 1932-33
Honors: All-SEC and All-American, 1932-33

Another candidate for best athlete in school history, Johnson was one of Rupp's first All-Americans and the first Wildcat to letter in four sports in the same year (basketball, football, baseball and track). He played minor league baseball but made his biggest mark in basketball and football, coaching both sports at Morehead State Teachers College, where he is the school's all-time victories leader in both. Morehead named its gym after Johnson, who retired from coaching in 1953 but returned in 1963 to coach rival Marshall. Soon, the winner of the annual Morehead-Marshall game received the Ellis Johnson Trophy. He died in 1990 at age 79.

HARRY LANCASTER

Years lettered: 1934-35, 1935-36, 1936-37
Assistant coach: 1947-69
Athletics director: 1969-75

No one was a more loyal Kentucky assistant than Lancaster, whose 22 years on Rupp's staff is a school record likely never to be broken. Little-known fact: Lancaster doubled as Kentucky's head baseball coach from 1951-65, winning 163 games—No. 2 in program history. Lancaster left Rupp's side in 1969 to become athletics director, causing no small amount of discomfort three years later when Rupp reached the state's mandatory retirement age of 70 and unhappily had to surrender his post. Lancaster retired in 1975 and healed his rift with Rupp before Rupp's death in 1977. Eight years later, when Lancaster died in 1985, he was buried a few feet away from Rupp at the Lexington Cemetery.

CAWOOD LEDFORD

Voice of the Wildcats: 1953-1992
Honors: Member, Naismith Basketball Hall of Fame;
retired jersey (no number)

It may be Rupp's arena, but it's Cawood's Court. That's the official name of the playing surface at Rupp Arena, where Ledford's baritone became synonymous with UK basketball during his 39 years as voice of the Wildcats. Ledford's career started and ended with bangs. His first game was Cliff Hagan's 51-point outburst in Kentucky's 1953-54 opener, its first contest since canceling the previous season. Ledford's last game ended with The Shot by Duke's Christian Laettner in the 1992 NCAA Tournament. In between he crafted the career that prompted the *Lexington Herald-Leader* in 1999 to select Ledford among the state's 50 most significant sports figures of the 20th century. Ledford was the only media member to make the list. Two years after his retirement he became the fifth broadcaster inducted into the media wing of the Naismith Basketball Hall of Fame. By then Oscar Cawood Ledford had returned to his hometown near Cawood, Kentucky—he was named for the town, not vice versa—to be with his wife, Frances, and their 49 miniature horses. He was 75 when he died in September 2001, three months before the hardwood floor at Rupp Arena would be named in his honor.

PAUL McBRAYER

Years lettered: 1927-28, 1928-29, 1929-30
Honors: All-American 1929-30

A man can be measured in many ways, but here's one way to get a grasp on McBrayer's impact: He kept getting things named in his honor. There's the coliseum at Eastern Kentucky, which in 1988 was renamed the Paul S. McBrayer Arena; the annual Kentucky basketball reunion dinner during homecoming festivities, which for 37 years was called "The McBrayer Dinner;" and the annual basketball reunion at Eastern Kentucky, which was called "The McBrayer Family." What did Paul McBrayer do to earn such admiration? He was an All-American at Kentucky and a nine-year assistant under Rupp before serving in World War II. He later was the EKU head coach for 16 seasons, setting the school's career record with 219 wins. He died in 1998 at age 89.

LAWRENCE AND LOUIS McGINNIS

Years lettered: Lawrence: 1927-28, 1928-29, 1929-30
Louis: 1928-29, 1929-30, 1930-31
Honors (Louis): All American, 1929-30)

The Wildcats' famed McGinnis brothers were known as "Big" and "Little," with Big Lawrence serving as team captain in 1929 and Little Louis earning All-American honors in 1930. Lawrence became a well-known coach at three Kentucky high schools, winning 467 games and the 1949 state championship while at Owensboro High. That team was led by Cliff Hagan, a future Kentucky star and athletics director. Lawrence McGinnis was 79 when he died in 1987. Louis McGinnis, who became a mortician in Lexington, was 93 when he died in 2003.

JAMES PARK

Years lettered: 1913-14; head coach 1915-16

He did a little of everything in college—playing football, baseball and basketball—and did a little bit more after school. Park pitched for the St. Louis Browns in the major leagues, going 4-5 with a 3.02 ERA from 1915-17. Between the 1915 and '16 seasons he coached the Kentucky basketball team to an 8-6 record, then served in the U.S. Army Air Corps during World War I. After his return to Lexington in the 1920s he served two years as a state representative and two decades as Fayette County's prosecuting attorney. He lost his 1944 bid for the U.S. Senate, perhaps because he was too nice for such a cut-throat political race. Park's former law partner, William H. Townsend, once said that Park was such a gentleman that he received a Christmas card from a prisoner on death row—a prisoner Park had put there as prosecutor. Park died in 1970 at age 78.

JACK TINGLE

**Years lettered: 1943-44, 1944-45, 1945-46, 1946-47
Honors: All-American and All-SEC 1946-47;
All-SEC 1943-44, 1944-45, 1945-46**

Few Kentucky basketball players won more honors than Tingle, whose immortality on the court was no match for the cancer that killed him at the shockingly young age of 33. Despite a badly broken left arm from a childhood fall that never healed properly, Tingle became one of just three Wildcats to earn first-team All-SEC honors all four years he lettered, as he did from 1944-47. In an era of the two-handed set shot, Tingle's right-handed release helped him become a two-time All-American and spend two seasons in the NBA before he came home in 1950. Tingle coached at Hiseville High School and worked in the photoengraving department of the *Louisville Courier-Journal* before being diagnosed with cancer in 1957. He told few people of the severity of the illness, which killed him in 1958.

Where Have You Gone?

CHARLES HURT

Nicknames clung to Charles Hurt like the biceps that inspired them. He was called "The Big Hurt" and "Atlas" during his career as a Kentucky power forward from 1979-83, but if the Wildcats were to give him a nickname today, it would be more appropriate to call him "The Recluse."

Charles Hurt, one of the most popular players in Kentucky history, has willingly dropped off the Kentucky radar.

"We had our twentieth reunion [in 2003] and he didn't make it," says former Kentucky center Melvin Turpin. "Nobody could get ahold of him. Everybody was asking where he was, but he's been really hard to find. I didn't know what to tell anybody."

Tell them this: After serving Big Blue Nation so ferociously, Charles Hurt went on to serve his red, white and blue nation with even greater passion.

Hurt enlisted in the U.S. Army in 1987 and made a career of it, rising to the rank of Master Sergeant nearly 17 years later. Along the way, Hurt had been stationed in places like Germany, Kuwait and Korea, while also serving at domestic bases in Augusta, Georgia, and El Paso, Texas.

While other Kentucky players have cashed in on their fame, parlaying their name recognition in the Bluegrass State into public office or successful careers in sales or coaching, Hurt went the other direction. He chose a job that pays peanuts, a job that on a bad day can mean you're not going home—ever again.

"Thinking back on it, it was a decision that I consciously made," Hurt says. "I'd done something there at the university that was enjoyable and ful-

CHARLES HURT

Years lettered: 1979-80, 1980-81, 1981-82, 1982-83
Career totals: 786 points, 496 rebounds, 104 assists, 19 blocks

filling, but I don't think there was anything else I could do more honorable than serving my country."

Over the years Hurt has received a handful of overtures from the University of Kentucky to return to Rupp Arena and claim his rightful place in Wildcat Lore, if only to be recognized for a moment at halftime of a game. Every time Hurt has declined, though he says it's nothing personal.

"It's just the way I wanted it," he says. "Kentucky basketball was a big part of my life, but that was years ago. Not that I'm not a huge fan—don't get me wrong—but you move on. You get a family, and that becomes a priority. Definitely what I'm doing now, that's my priority. I remember all the guys and that's great, but I just moved on."

Before we move on with the rest of Charles Hurt's story, let us remember one of the most unsung players in Kentucky history. Hurt played a pivotal role in nearly every one of his 124 games at Kentucky and finished his career as the school's all-time leader in field goal accuracy. To this day his 59.3 percent career shooting from the floor ranks seventh in the SEC, yet Hurt never made the All-SEC first, second or third teams. In his day he wasn't even considered the best Hurt in the conference, falling behind the more flamboyant Bobby Lee Hurt of Alabama.

Yet it was Charles Hurt who was the backbone of Joe B. Hall's teams in the early 1980s. He averaged 6.3 points and four rebounds for his career, modest numbers that belied his impact on the floor as a defender and intimidating presence. When future NBA players like Turpin and point guard Dirk Minniefield were leading Kentucky to back-to-back victories against Ohio State and Indiana early in the 1981-82 season, it was Hurt who inspired the *Sports Illustrated* headline that Kentucky was "putting the Big Hurt into the Big Ten."

When Kentucky went into Auburn on February 12, 1983, to take on Auburn's double-chuck tandem of Chuck Person and Charles Barkley, it was Hurt who was given the task of guarding Barkley. Today he's recognized as one of the NBA's greatest 50 players of all time, but on February 12, 1983, Barkley was merely another player in Hurt's way. At one point, as the players banged under the basket, the six-foot-six, 215-pound Hurt bounced the 6-6, 260-pound Barkley into the third row. Kentucky won 71-69, avenging a loss the previous season at Auburn in which Barkley had finished with 18 points and 12 rebounds.

It was that kind of thing that earned Hurt a place in the Louisville *Courier-Journal*'s turn-of-the-century look at Kentucky basketball. Hurt was the first player named to the newspaper's "Fearless Five," joining Winston Bennett, Rick Robey, Frank Ramsey and Allen Feldhaus.

Still fearless, Hurt has stayed in the army throughout various Middle East upheavals—Kuwait, Afghanistan, Iraq, etc.—although he could get out whenever he wants. As of his 17th year in the service, Hurt was stationed at Fort Hood near El Paso and had yet to see combat, though he was playing a supporting role to the troops in Iraq. He was working in the army's version of Information Technology, keeping the troops connected with the army leadership.

"I'm an information systems chief, so we do all the networking—computer networking, things of that nature," Hurt says. "We do communicating all over world."

As for Hurt, he believes his little slice of heaven is in northeast Georgia, where he still owns the house he had lived in while stationed at Fort Gordon, a few miles outside Augusta. After hitting 20 years in the U.S. Army, Hurt says he will consider retiring from the service and moving his wife and children back to Augusta.

By then Hurt will be in his late 40s and looking to start his second career. He wants to be a teacher.

"I've got a plan," he says. "I told my wife at 20 years [in the army], that's my magic number because I want to get into school teaching. I expect I'll teach maybe 10 or 15 years—do that, and then completely retire."

Hurt doesn't see leaving the army for the classroom as getting away from responsibility. Just the opposite: he sees teaching as another way of serving his country, this time from a more proactive standpoint than the military.

"I'm looking at teaching kids in their formative years—sixth, seventh or eighth grade," Hurt says. "You'll see me in a middle school. That seems to be where there's more of a need for influence."

Where Have You Gone?

LARRY PURSIFUL

As a player, Larry Pursiful was ahead of his time—a long-range scorer who played a quarter of a century before college basketball added the three-point arc.

As a minister, Pursiful says he was right on time: God's time.

"God found a way to call me into the ministry late in my life," says Pursiful, the minister of outreach for Westport Road Baptist Church in Louisville. "There was a period of four, five months that I felt the call. I was 47 at the time, and in the shoe business."

Before he got into the foot business, Pursiful had a hand in a lot of businesses. Best as he knew how, he was trying to find his way after his basketball career had ended in 1964.

At Kentucky, Pursiful had been one of the most pure outside shooters the program has known. He shot 51 percent from the floor and 82 percent from the foul line as a senior, averaging 19.1 points on the Wildcats' 23-3 team in 1962. Cotton Nash was that team's best player but Pursiful was its unsung hero, his shooting ability freeing Nash to work inside and out to the tune of 23.4 points per game. The next season, without Pursiful to keep defenses from ganging up on him, Nash's scoring dropped to 20.6 points per game.

But we're getting off track …not unlike Pursiful in the early 1960s.

After college Pursiful was selected by Chicago in the eighth round of the 1962 NBA Draft, but he didn't stick. Even in 1962, a slight shooting guard had a difficult time finding a home in the NBA, and Pursiful was definitely smallish at six-foot-one, 165 pounds. He landed with the Phillips 66ers of the old National Industrial Basketball League, a league that gave ex-col-

124

lege players in the industrial field a place to earn a few extra bucks. The Phillips 66ers, wearing the cutting-edge sneakers of the day (Chuck Taylors by Converse), played teams like the Denver Truckers, Peoria Caterpillars and Akron Goodyear.

Pursiful retired in 1964, unsure what to do next. He had been a Christian since he was ten years old, but he says the pull of the ministry wasn't getting through to him.

"God knew what he was doing," Pursiful says. "I wasn't ready to go into ministry. I was too interested in other things."

After spending one year each as a coach at Harrisburg (Kentucky) High and Larue County High in Hodgenville, Kentucky, Pursiful meandered through the private sector. He spent two years as a sales representative for Phillips and two more in banking, then bought a hardware store. Meanwhile, his wife had opened a shoe store in a Louisville mall that became a success. Pursiful had been spending more and more of his time with the shoe store when, at age 47, he says he felt the calling of the ministry.

Pursiful took some classes at a local seminary, then became an associate pastor at a local church for eight years before moving to Westport Road Baptist in 1996. Along the way Pursiful incorporated basketball into his outreach.

That meant little things like playing in the church league, and it meant bigger things like founding a touring team that has made basketball-oriented mission trips to 12 countries and 13 states. Pursiful played in the church league until he was 62, when he finally hung up his Chuck Taylors.

"My jumper never left me," he says. "But I couldn't get open any more."

Pursiful's traveling team ministry, founded as the Kentucky Baptist Sports Crusaders before changing its name to Sports Reach, made its first international trip in 1989 to Kenya. There, the Crusaders posted a 12-1 record, though the number from that trip that would matter most to Pursiful is 600—the estimated number of Kenyans who were baptized thanks to basketball.

Over the years Sports Reach has mushroomed into a ministry that conducts basketball, softball, soccer, cheerleading and baseball camps around the country. It also sponsors a traveling team that plays exhibition games in prisons and against NCAA and NAIA teams. Sports Reach's professional division, the Kentucky Reach, plays in the World Basketball Association that was created in 2004 as a minor league just below the NBDL.

He was born too early, Larry Pursiful. Not only did he miss out on the three-point arc, but he missed out on the chance to play for the Kentucky Reach. The Reach probably could have used a shooter like Pursiful, who most famously heated up during the 1961 University of Kentucky Invitational Tournament when he scored 20 of his team's first 23 points in a victory against Tennessee. Pursiful ended that season by leading the Wildcats in scoring in both their 1962 NCAA Tournament games, with 26 points in a victory against Butler and 21 points in a loss to Ohio State. That earned Pursiful a spot on the All-Mideast Regional team, despite Kentucky's elimination.

Ask Pursiful for his Kentucky basketball memories, and he doesn't go into length about any of those exploits. He doesn't talk much about his basketball days at Kentucky any more, even as it has intersected with ministry. For example, it is from other sources that you would learn about the Crusaders and about Sports Reach, and about his officiating role at the 1998 funeral of Esther Rupp, Adolph's widow.

Pursiful is similarly humble around members of Westport Road Baptist, many of whom don't know they have a former Kentucky great in their midst. Pursiful says his college career only seemed to be a conversational point in the days when he would go to the church's gym and shoot, wowing players half his age with a stroke that was pure—even as Pursiful was nearing 60. After all, Pursiful did score nearly 1,000 points in his final two seasons at Kentucky.

"The average age of our members is 33," he says. "They probably don't remember that stuff. That's not important any more, anyway."

Where Have You Gone?

RICHIE FARMER

Richie Farmer didn't know exactly what he was going to do with his life, but he knew he had options. It was the summer of 1992, and Farmer had just concluded his storybook career at Kentucky—storybook in the sense that Farmer, already a teenage legend around Kentucky thanks to his high school heroics in the boys state tournament, had gone on to score nearly 1,000 points for the Wildcats and help John Pelphrey, Deron Feldhaus and the rest of The Unforgettables come within a Christian Laettner miracle of the 1992 Final Four.

After that, Farmer had options. He could have become a professional basketball player, though not in the United States. Too small, too slow, too this, too that. But clubs overseas were always looking for a high-scoring American, and that was Farmer, a six-foot guard who had needed just 11 shots from the floor to hang 28 points on Notre Dame in January 1992. Teams in Germany and Australia wanted him. So that was an option.

On the other hand, Farmer knew he could make more than the $50,000 or $60,000 the foreign clubs were offering by staying home and cashing in on his popularity. Richie Farmer was then, and is now, one of the most popular players ever to play Kentucky basketball. The love affair began when he was at Clay County High School, where he played in a record five Sweet 16 classics, starting with eighth grade and ending as a senior when he scored 51 points in the 1989 state title game. Throw in his role in the rebuilding of Kentucky Wildcat basketball from 1990-92, and he was a walking ATM. Personal appearances, book deals, autograph shows—you name it, and he could have done it.

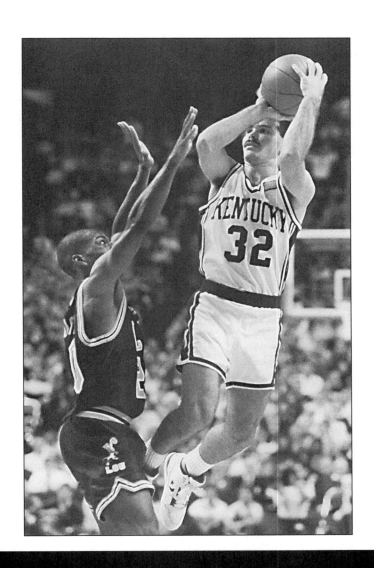

RICHIE FARMER

Years lettered: 1988-89, 1989-90, 1990-91, 1991-92
Honors: retired jersey No. 32
Career totals: 898 points, 184 rebounds, 184 assists,
147 three-pointers (9th in UK history)

Regarding his future, about the only thing Farmer knew for sure was this: No politics.

"I swore I'd never be in politics," he says. "I always had the impression it was dirty, nasty and corrupt, and that's not something I wanted to be a part of."

This passes for irony, because Farmer said those words from his office in Frankfort, Kentucky, where he was in the middle of a four-year term as state agriculture commissioner.

That's an elected position, don't you know. That makes Farmer a bonafide politician. More than a year after his November 2003 election, he still sounded as if he couldn't believe it himself.

"If you'd told me two years ago I'd be holding a constitutional office, I'd have thought you were as crazy as a loon," he says. "This is the one thing I said I'd never do."

Farmer took a meandering path into politics. Right off the bat he turned down those opportunities to play professionally overseas, letting that epic 104-103 loss to Laettner and Duke in the 1992 East Region title game serve as his final game of organized basketball. For one thing, it beat finishing his career in a half-empty gym halfway across the world. For another, he simply didn't want to leave Kentucky in the summer of 1992.

After graduating from Kentucky with a double major in agriculture economics and agribusiness management, Farmer returned to Clay County. There he wrote a book, an autobiography that sold enough copies that it required a second printing. And there, at the urging of his matchmaking aunt, he went on a blind date with a young woman from Leslie County. That went well enough, too; Richie and Rebecca Farmer have been married for almost a decade and have three sons: Trey, Thomas and Tate.

"Sticking around definitely paid off," Farmer says.

Sure it did. He also went into business, first in sports marketing where he marketed a handful of well-known Kentucky athletes, including himself, and then into a financial planning partnership with his father. They were doing quite well in late 2002 when Farmer's father, Richard, entered his son's office and rocked his son's world.

"Son," he told Richie, "I know you're a good person and have a good heart, and I know the way you feel about politics. But if everyone who was a good person felt the way you do about politics, who'd be left to run our state and run our country? The greatest gift you can give your boys is to get involved on a statewide level and make this a better place for them to grow up."

Richie Farmer remembers his response, and he remembers it verbatim: "Man, what did I do to you?"

Farmer tried to dismiss what his father had said but couldn't. Strangely enough, rumors had been swirling for months that he was going to run for public office. Farmer had heard those rumors, and he had laughed them off. But he couldn't laugh off what his father had said.

"I filed on the last day you could file [in January 2003], and right up to then it was not an easy decision for me," he says. "It wasn't something I had aspired to do—not like my basketball career, where it was a passion and a dream. Entering politics was something I'd fought really hard with. I thought it over, talked to a lot of my mentors, got a lot of opinions, and finally I decided, why not?"

Farmer considered a number of positions before settling on state agriculture commissioner, where Democrat Billy Ray Smith had reached his term limit. Farmer ran on the Republican ticket opposite Democrat Alice Woods Baesler, whose husband—get ready for more irony—was also a former Kentucky basketball player. Scotty Baesler had played for the Wildcats from 1961-63, averaging 10.9 points and a team-best 4.3 assists as a junior in 1962.

For Farmer, running for state agriculture commissioner made sense on the most basic of levels.

"Growing up in rural Kentucky, I know how important agriculture is to the state of Kentucky—and to the world," he says. "It affects every single family, every single day. I said if I'm going to do it, I want to be in the forefront, and I want to be involved in something that affects people's lives of this state."

Farmer's goal was to raise the awareness level around the state of the importance of Kentucky's agriculture sector. Being a famous basketball player at the high school and collegiate levels, was part of his platform. He doesn't apologize for that.

"Being a former Kentucky basketball player, that's something that touches every single family in this state," Farmer says. "People are passionate about Kentucky basketball. The name recognition, and just being out there and talking about things going on in agriculture, we've definitely raised people's awareness of how important agriculture is.

"A lot of [skeptics] at first thought, 'This guy's a ball player and name recognition got him elected,' but now they're saying that I have ideas and ambitions to do good things for agriculture. I won't be naïve and say people still don't associate me with basketball, because they do. People in this state have associated me with basketball basically all my life. But that's not really a bad thing. We can take that and use it in a positive way for agriculture. I think I'll always be remembered as a Kentucky basketball player, but I think I'll be judged on how I did as agriculture commissioner."

Unless he climbs higher up the political ladder. Senator Farmer? Governor Farmer? If the reviews are positive after his first term as state agriculture commissioner, Farmer would be in a position to run for any office in the state. He knows that, but he doesn't want to go there. Not now. There's still work to be done in agriculture.

"I'm just trying to do the best job I can do," he says. "I'll equate it to basketball—it's like taking it one game at a time. The way I've approached this is to do the best job I can do and evaluate the situation when that time comes. If I do a good job, and it's something I really enjoy, maybe I'll seek another term or maybe I'll go home [to Clay County] or maybe I'll do something else in politics. I want to be the best agriculture commissioner that Kentucky has ever had, and I feel like if I go at it that way, I'll have my options when it's over."

As always.

WINSTON BENNETT

Winston Bennett wanted to be a coach, but not just any coach. He wanted to coach a high-level college program, or perhaps a team in the NBA. That was his dream.

Outside the cocoon of Kentucky basketball, however, Bennett has seen how a nightmare can be more powerful than any dream.

Bennett was a star forward for the Wildcats in the mid-1980s, and after a five-year professional career he quickly became a star coaching prospect. That was good. That was his goal.

Bennett's coaching career first began to sink at about the same time it should have zoomed skyward. After four years as an assistant to Kentucky coach Rick Pitino, including the Wildcats' 1996 national championship season, Bennett followed Pitino to the Boston Celtics in 1997. Tall and handsome, Bennett struck a striking figure on an NBA sideline. Only 32 years old and with the credibility that comes from NBA playing experience, it wasn't difficult to imagine Bennett coaching his own NBA team in the near future.

"I always said I wanted to be a head coach at the professional level," Bennett said in 1997, when he joined the Celtics. "This is going to look good on the resume."

This wouldn't look so good: Bennett was forced to resign before that 1997-98 season was finished after the Celtics discovered he had been having an affair with a student of nearby Brandeis University.

In an interview with the Louisville *Courier-Journal*, Bennett acknowledged his sexual addiction, which psychologists say can be every bit as overpowering as alcoholism or drug addiction. Bennett sought counseling, rec-

WINSTON BENNETT

Years lettered: 1983-84, 1984-85, 1986-87, 1987-88
Honors: All-SEC 1985-86, 1987-88
Career totals: 1,399 points (18th in UK history), 799 rebounds
(10th in UK history), 153 assists, 123 steals

onciled with his wife and in 1999 was working again. Pitino had rehired him as a Celtics scout.

One year later, Kentucky State University offered Bennett the chance to get back into coaching. Kentucky State, a Division II school in Frankfort, Kentucky, wasn't the coaching job Bennett had dreamed of as a younger man, but in May 2000 he was 35 years old. Job offers weren't exactly falling into his lap.

He said yes.

Then he ran into more trouble.

During a sweeping investigation of Kentucky State that began with an inquiry into the track and field program, the NCAA determined Bennett had actually begun recruiting for Kentucky State before becoming an official employee of the school, and therefore wasn't authorized to recruit. The NCAA also determined Bennett had observed offseason pick-up games involving his players with other students, another NCAA no-no.

The university sent Bennett a letter of reprimand and required him to attend an NCAA compliance seminar and then work with school officials to train his staff members. The school also reduced his recruiting opportunities for the 2001-02 academic year.

Bennett kept his job, and regarding wins and losses, he did his job. Kentucky State wasn't a great basketball school, but three years into his tenure the Thorobreds had won more than they had lost—going 44-43 in that time—and Bennett seemed to be settling into his leadership role.

And then came his biggest (professional) mistake yet.

From a marketability standpoint, and to borrow a baseball metaphor, Bennett had entered the 2003-04 season with two strikes against him: his admitted sexual addiction while at Boston, and his NCAA violations while with Kentucky State.

Strike Three came on October 30, 2003. That was the day Bennett struck one of his players in the face at least twice, according to court records. One week later, and only eight days before the 2003-04 season opener, Kentucky State fired Bennett.

"I felt ... that this was the right thing to do," Kentucky State athletics director Derrick Ramsey said in announcing Bennett's dismissal. "One of the prime responsibilities I have at this institution is to protect the welfare of student-athletes."

According to several witnesses, Bennett had failed to do that during an early-morning practice on Oct. 30. The incident began at about 7 a.m., with Thorobreds guard Ricky Green jumping out of bounds to save a loose ball and throwing it off a teammate's face. Bennett immediately confronted

Green, accusing him of intentionally throwing the ball at his teammate, Green would later tell the Kentucky State Police Department.

What happened next is up to interpretation. At least three people— Green, assistant coach Tom Patterson and an anonymous witness believed to be another player—told police that Bennett had hit Green, and that Green hadn't struck back.

Green's official statement to campus police painted a frightening picture of the six-foot-seven, 260-pound Bennett attacking someone nearly seven inches shorter and 70 pounds lighter: "[Bennett] then walked up on me, grabbing my shirt and hitting me several times in the face until my nose bled heavily and tearing my shirt off," Green wrote.

In Bennett's official statement to authorities later that morning, he said, "We both began to throw blows at each other."

Bennett's statement continued: "My intention has never been to hurt Ricky. Ricky is a kid that's on his own. I am trying my best to help him become a better man. He has to understand he can't do what he wants to do when he wants to do it."

Bennett initially would plead not guilty to any charges, but on February 24, 2004 he pleaded guilty to assault in the fourth degree. He was sentenced to perform 200 hours of community service and to get counseling in anger management, with a jail term of 90 days to be imposed if he didn't meet those requirements within six months.

Within ten days Bennett had begun his counseling. He started his community service even earlier, doing janitorial and other work for G.O. Ministries in Louisville on February 29, 2004. Bennett would volunteer for 18 consecutive days, often for eight hours at a time, at three places: G.O. Ministries, the Christ Temple Christian Life Center, and The Lord's Kitchen. There, according to court documents, his duties included serving food to the homeless and cleaning up after them.

By April 15, Bennett had put in his 200 hours of service. On April 26, he had finished receiving his counseling. On May 25, 2004, his guilty plea was set aside, the charges dismissed with prejudice.

Bennett didn't speak that day at the Franklin County Courthouse, located roughly one mile from his former office at Kentucky State University. He had said enough in his final sentence of that statement to campus police seven months earlier, when he said of his altercation with Green, "I regret that we ever started fighting each other."

He might well regret it the rest of his life. It's possible another school will give Bennett a coaching job, although probably not as a head coach. If he wants to stay in the game, Bennett's best bet likely would be to use his professional contacts—he played three seasons in the NBA, one season in the

Continental Basketball Association and one season in Italy—to get a job in that realm. Rehabilitation can happen, but for a coach with three high-profile and vastly different missteps, it will take time.

Bennett declined to be interviewed for this book. He didn't return messages left with his Louisville-based attorney, Chris Meinhart, and with Program Resources, a Louisville-based speaker's bureau that represents him.

Bennett was offering his services as a motivational speaker before his dismissal from Kentucky State, and he was offering his services afterward as well. In some ways, he has much to offer. Bennett has made mistakes, which would give his message credibility, and he was always a skillful speaker, a persuasive and passionate man who was a favorite of reporters as a Kentucky player. The Jefferson County Sheriff's Department invited Bennett to make an anti-drug plea to the community, a message he delivered with aplomb. Back then he dreamed of becoming a head coach at a place like Kentucky, or perhaps in the NBA.

Maybe that dream has died. Maybe it has only been delayed. Only time will tell if Bennett is meant to accomplish something greater than his career totals of 1,399 points and 799 rebounds as a Kentucky Wildcat from 1984-88.

Where Have You Gone?

BOB
GUYETTE

Former Kentucky center Bob Guyette has a remarkable story, a touching story, but there's also a hint of the macabre, so forgive us—we're starting his story with something gruesome:

The guy with the knife in his eye.

Guyette is a plastic surgeon in Phoenix—and at six foot nine, perhaps the tallest plastic surgeon in the world—so he sees facial trauma on a regular basis. The worst thing he's seen, though, was the young man who was brought into the hospital where Guyette once worked in Birmingham, Alabama.

"He had this huge knife sticking out of his eyeball," Guyette says. "He came into the emergency room after a drug deal went bad. Someone had taken this huge knife and rammed it in there, but he was wide awake, talking to us. We hammered on this knife to get it out, but it was tricky because we didn't know if we'd nicked the carotid artery and he'd bleed to death when the knife came out. It turned out about as good as it could have—he lost sight in the eye, but he survived.

"The next day when I went in to see him, he wasn't worried about his eye, but his mom, because he said his mom was going to kill him. He wanted me to keep her out of the room, but I couldn't do it. She closed the door, and I heard her raise her voice. I kept on walking, because I thought she probably had some good advice for him."

Guyette knows a good parent when he sees one, probably because he's been one himself. The oldest of Bob and Regina Guyette's three sons, Rob, graduated from the Naval Academy with a major in aerospace engineering. He ended the 2004 calendar year as a U.S. Marine in Quantico, Virginia,

BOB GUYETTE

Years lettered: 1972-73, 1973-74, 1974-75
Career totals: 758 points, 541 rebounds, 74 assists

awaiting a transfer to Pensacola where he was to learn how to fly F-18s. From there, Rob Guyette expects to be sent to the Middle East.

"I'm proud of Rob and everyone he's training with," says Bob Guyette. "They believe in more than just themselves. They want to be part of something bigger than themselves."

Guyette's middle son, Kevin, is a pitcher for the University of Arizona. He was drafted out of high school by the Seattle Mariners and was the No. 3 starter on Arizona's 2004 team that reached the College World Series, but his baseball ability isn't the best thing about Kevin. This is: After his freshman season at Georgia Tech, he left Atlanta to be closer to his father. In 2002, Bob Guyette had learned the tumor in his tonsils was cancerous. Kevin transferred to Arizona, two hours away in Tucson, and wrote his father a supportive, two-page letter that Bob still can't discuss without breaking into tears. When Kevin pitched in Rosenblatt Stadium in Omaha, Nebraska, for the 2004 College World Series, Bob was there.

Bob survived the tonsil cancer, and he plans to stick around long enough to watch his youngest son, Brian, become a pilot. Brian was an Arizona all-state goal keeper in high school, and in the fall of 2004 he began classes as a freshman at Air Force. He planned to play soccer and position himself to fly jets.

"We've had an amazing run," Bob says. "Having these boys, watching them grow up, being proud ... it's been amazing."

Indeed, life didn't simply peak for Guyette at Kentucky—though he was a pretty fair player on some pretty fair teams. His best individual season was in 1973-74, when he was the team's No. 2 scorer (behind Kevin Grevey) at 12.7 points per game, and led the Wildcats with 7.9 rebounds per game. Guyette played on his best team the following season, a typical Kentucky juggernaut at 26-5, though the arrival of freshman big men Rick Robey and Mike Phillips meant fewer minutes for him. Kentucky lost 92-85 to UCLA in the 1975 NCAA championship game, with Guyette producing 16 points and seven rebounds against a Bruins front line of Dave Meyers, Marques Johnson and Richard Washington.

Kansas City of the NBA drafted Guyette in the third round in 1975, but he landed with a professional team in Spain. He played overseas for five years, investing his earnings into duplexes back home in Lexington, Kentucky—renting and ultimately selling the real estate to provide for his family while he went to dental and medical school.

He first tried to go to medical school in Spain, but that was derailed by the death of a dictator.

"I had learned enough Spanish to get by, and in the spring of '76 I enrolled in medical school in Barcelona," Guyette says. "Francisco Franco had just died, so when I went to class that first day they were speaking another language, the Barcelona-area language. I didn't understand the language, let alone biochemistry. Biochemistry is tough enough in English. That was a short career of medical school. I lasted three classes."

Guyette eventually went to dental school at Kentucky, but one of the principal things he learned was that he wanted to be more than a dentist. At the time, only a handful of U.S. colleges offered medical school with a specialty of oral-maxillofacial surgery. One was Alabama, which is how Guyette ended up attending a rival SEC school. It worked out fine. Guyette was a resident at Alabama-Birmingham—where he worked on the guy with the knife stuck in his eye—before moving to Phoenix.

In 15 years as a surgeon, Guyette figures he has operated on close to 20,000 faces, some of them belonging to actors, athletes and their spouses. The weather in Phoenix doesn't fluctuate a great deal, though Guyette says he can tell what season it is based on the procedures he is most asked to perform.

"Winter is nice," he says. "There's the influx of snowbirds, and our percentage of facial cosmetic surgery increases significantly—eyelids, nasal, that type of thing. Summer is more reconstructive: jaws, facial deformities. We do procedures to realign facial bones from a cosmetic and functional standpoint. Throughout the year we do trauma surgery, cleft lip and palate, laser surgery. What I like about the practice is the diversity. There is no typical day."

Twice a year Guyette takes staff members to Guaymas, Mexico, a port city of about 150,000 people. There, as missionary work for his church in Phoenix, he spends four days offering free surgery.

"In Mexico a lot of people don't have access to good medical treatment," he says. "People with deformities are ostracized from society down there, so helping folks restore normal appearance makes a huge difference in their lives."

Where Have You Gone?

ROB
LOCK

Fate wasn't all that kind to Rob Lock at Kentucky.
Though he was a productive player who averaged 10.9 points and 6.5 rebounds as a senior in 1988, fans with crazy-high expectations weren't thrilled with Lock's workmanlike career. Though he was never connected to any wrongdoing, Lock suffered along with the rest of the program when Kentucky was forced to vacate its 1988 SEC championship after an NCAA investigation of teammates Chris Mills and Eric Manuel.

After all that, fate owed Rob Lock.

Less than two decades later, consider the debt paid in full.

"I've got it pretty good," Lock says.

Yes, he does. Lock married a model-musician-television personality named Valerie Still, whom Kentucky fans might remember as the all-time scoring and rebounding leader—man or woman—in Wildcats history. In 1996 they had a son named Aaron Still Lock who is expected to grow beyond seven feet tall, and even though he hasn't shown much of an interest in basketball, he is growing up healthy and happy.

And then there's the family business. Get a load of this: Lock is a barnstorming bi-plane pilot, a throwback to the 1920s when flying was such a novelty that people would pay the princely sum of one dollar for a short ride in the open-cockpit contraption.

A fluke, all of it.

"It's amazing how it all turned out," Lock says. "I never thought any of this was possible."

Both Lock's marriage and career have been the result of plain old good luck. Lock knows, but he's not about to give either back.

ROB LOCK

Years lettered: 1984-85, 1985-86, 1986-87, 1987-88
Career totals: 691 points, 475 rebounds,
83 blocks (9th in UK history)

Though they attended the same college, Valerie Still was five years older than Lock and was long gone by the time he arrived in Lexington in the fall of 1984. At that point Still was in Italy, where she played professionally, dabbled in modeling and sang at a nightclub outside Milan. She returned briefly to Lexington in 1986, during Lock's sophomore year, and they met at Memorial Coliseum. Or so he says.

"Valerie doesn't remember [meeting me]," Lock says.

No problem. Several years later, after he had spent the 1988-89 season with the NBA's Los Angeles Clippers, Lock himself turned up in Italy to play professionally. There was a club outside Milan where most of the American players hung out, and Lock was invited to hear this tall, beautiful singer. Lock didn't go.

"I didn't go out that much," he says.

Again, no problem. By the early 1990s, Still was such a popular figure in Italy that a local television station hired her as a reporter. On one assignment, she was sent to interview Darryl Dawkins, the backboard-shattering center from America who was playing for the Italian team in Milan. While she was in town for the story, Still was introduced to one of Dawkins' teammates, a former Kentucky basketball player named Rob Lock.

They were married in 1995.

"She's great, the best thing that ever happened to me," says Lock. "You look at how it all played out, and it's pretty obvious we were meant to be together."

When Lock retired from basketball in 1996 the couple returned to the United States and decided to settle down in Lexington. Valerie thought she was retired, too, but fate would have something to say about that. Two new professional leagues for women were in the process of forming in the United States, and Still was a hot commodity, though her age was closer to 40 than 30. Still came out of retirement to play for the Columbus Quest of the American Basketball League, and the family—Aaron was about six months old—moved from Lexington to a hotel room in Columbus, Ohio, for the season.

Thanks to their dual-career savings from Italy and Still's salary with the Quest, the family didn't need Lock to work. He stayed with Aaron.

Meanwhile, in California ...

"My dad was an airplane mechanic [near Fresno], and he was always looking through trade magazines," Lock says. "One day he saw a couple of old bi-planes for sale in Portland, Oregon. They were packed away in a trac-tor-trailer up there."

Having spent his childhood around planes, Lock had begun flying as an adolescent and dreamed of being an airline pilot. By age 14 he had grown to six foot eight and figured he might need to look for another career. Basketball was it, though he earned his pilot's license shortly after graduating from Kentucky.

While Valerie played for the Quest and Rob played Mr. Mom for Aaron, he began to wonder about his next career move. That's when Bob Lock called his son and told him about the bi-planes for sale in Oregon: Would Rob like to buy them?

"I told him to go take a look," Lock says. "I thought they might be a toy. There aren't many cockpits big enough for a six foot-10 pilot, but a bi-plane is one of them."

In late 1996 Lock's father drove a trailer up the Pacific coast and bought both bi-planes, though "bi-planes" was a generous description. Basically, they were bi-plane skeletons. No wings, no panels, just the metal framework.

Neither plane had been flown since the 1940s. One had lost its wings after crashing into a barn during an errant crop-dusting flight in 1942, while the other had caught fire in a wheat field in Yakima, Washington, in 1949. After landing someone had thrown a cigarette into the wheat, and soon flames destroyed the plane's fuselage.

Lock's father needed four years and help from a handy friend as well as a plane-restoration company, but in June 2000 he had the Yakima plane ready for flight. By that time Rob Lock had decided what he wanted to do with the planes: Return them to their original purpose, and sell plane rides to the public.

Valerie would handle the bookkeeping, Rob the flying. His father would be the mechanic, which left only the matter of naming the company. Lock settled on "Waldo Wright's Flying Service," getting the name by combining a popular 1975 movie title with the Wright Brothers. The movie, *The Great Waldo Pepper*, starred Robert Redford as a barnstorming bi-plane pilot.

Four years later, in mid-2004, Lock's father had the old crop-duster ready for flight. Two planes required two pilots, so Rob hired his father—a licensed pilot as well as a mechanic. Today Waldo Wright's Flying Service averages about 7,000 guest flights a year, and is recognized as the country's largest provider of open-cockpit flights. Lock spends the summer months in Ohio, working weekends in the Midwest, then heads to Florida for seven months to continue his flights in warm weather.

Valerie and Aaron come with him, of course. When Lock is in the air, Valerie takes care of Aaron.

Speaking of the little guy ...he's not so little. By age six, Aaron Lock was almost five feet tall and getting mentioned in a story by *ESPN The Magazine* that was determined to find "The Next Shaq." With doctors predicting Aaron's eventual height to reach seven foot one, Rob Lock admits to wondering what kind of basketball player Aaron could become—though he says any skill would come from his wife.

"I just gave him height," Lock says.

Aaron Lock has been given a lot more than that. He has accompanied his parents to their old stomping grounds, helping Rob and Wildcats cheerleaders form the last letter in "K-E-N-T-U-C-K-Y" during a men's game at Rupp Arena in January 2003. The next day he headed to midcourt at Memorial Coliseum while his mom had her jersey retired. Aaron also has accompanied his mother to the White House, where they met Hillary Clinton.

"He's a neat little boy," Lock says. "I used to wonder what kind of basketball player he could become, but now I just want him to become the best young man he can be."

Although Aaron doesn't enjoy basketball now, don't be surprised if he changes his mind and becomes a great player—for Kentucky, even.

Fate seems to like this family.

Where Have You Gone?

THAD JARACZ

Thad Jaracz is skeptical, and you can't blame him. His first reaction was that he'd rather not be interviewed for this book, or even included in this book.

Jaracz was a member of one of the more incredible teams not only in Kentucky history, but in college basketball history. It was 1965-66, and Kentucky coach Adolph Rupp's undersized, overachieving group was called "Rupp's Runts." Coming off a 15-10 season in 1964-65, those Wildcats weren't ranked in anyone's preseason Top 20—yet on the season's final day they were 27-1, champions of the SEC and participants in the 1966 NCAA championship game.

Nearly four decades later, each member of the starting five from that team has gone on to great success. Forward Pat Riley, the leading scorer in 1965-66, earned recognition as perhaps the finest NBA coach of his era. High-scoring guard Louie Dampier had a tremendous professional playing career, went into private business and has since become an NBA assistant coach. Larry Conley, an undersized forward at 6-3, is one of the South's most respected college basketball analysts. Tommy Kron has been a successful businessman in Louisville.

And Thad Jaracz, the awfully small 6-5 center and primary reason for the nickname "Rupp's Runts," went on to serve his country for 20 years in the U.S. Army, including stints in Korea and Germany.

There is honor in what those men have achieved after college, just as there was honor in what they achieved in 1965-66. Over the years, though, that 1966 NCAA title game between Kentucky and Texas Western has evolved from a championship event into a morality play. In various media

147

THAD JARACZ
(RIGHT)

Years lettered: 1965-66, 1966-67, 1967-68
Honors: All-SEC 1965-66
Career totals: 982 points, 626 rebounds, 68 assists

portraits, that game has grown into a microcosm not of Texas Western vs. Kentucky, but of good vs. evil.

Kentucky has not been portrayed as the good guys.

As if you didn't know ... that game pitted Rupp's all-white roster against a Texas Western team (now known as UTEP) that started five African-Americans. In an era of advancements in civil rights and integration, Kentucky was seen as behind the times. Three years later Rupp would sign his first African-American recruit, Tom Payne of Louisville, but of the two teams in the 1966 title game, Rupp's Wildcats were not viewed kindly.

History has done nothing to change that perspective.

Hence, Jaracz's uneasiness with his inclusion in this book. Too many times he has allowed himself to be interviewed for a media project only to find out that it was another rip job on Kentucky, Rupp or both.

"What kind of questions are you going to ask?" Jaracz wants to know.

Only questions about Thad Jaracz, he is told. No political agendas here—although Jaracz is asked what it has been like, over the years, to be a widely recognized member of one of the most (unfairly) maligned teams in college basketball history.

"It goes both ways," he says. "We get at least a couple of calls a year, somebody writing a book or doing a movie, and they want to make some point about something. The way I like to look at it is like this: As I look back on my life and the things I did, that's a season, being that successful, that means a lot to me. It still does, and I'm real proud of it. When all the other stuff gets lumped in on top of it, it makes you not think so warmly of that time."

Kentucky fans have warm memories of the spunky Jaracz. At 6-5 he was usually several inches shorter than his peers in the post, but he was almost always quicker and, at 230 pounds, at least as strong. That was enough for him to average 13.2 points and 7.5 rebounds as a sophomore in 1965-66, his most productive season with the Wildcats. Jaracz was named a third-team All-American that year, helping Kentucky win 23 consecutive games to open the season.

"You had a lot of bigger centers back then, but it was an era where they were really not as mobile and athletic as they are now," Jaracz says. "There were some great big, athletic centers—but not as a rule, not like they are now."

Jaracz ended his career with averages of 12 points and 7.6 rebounds per game, production that had the Boston Celtics take him with their fifth-round pick—No. 60 overall, the equivalent of a second-rounder in today's game. The Celtics released Jaracz but asked him to play in a secondary league just in case they needed him fresh and in shape, but in 1969 Jaracz was drafted into the U.S. Army. That was that.

As he did with basketball, Jaracz flung himself into his military career. He attended Officer Candidate School and received a commission, and when his two years in the service were finished he decided to stick around. He stayed in the service until 1990.

"I just really liked what I was doing," he says. "I liked working in leadership, having responsibility, and I really felt like most of the time what we were doing was important, and we were making a difference."

While reaching the rank of Lieutenant Colonel, Jaracz spent 21 years in the army, most unusually as the head of the ROTC department at the University of ... Louisville?

"It's funny how some things just fall out of the sky," Jaracz says. "I don't think I was sent there because someone had a sense of humor, but it really was a fun place to work. It was a nice school and everything, and I used to take a lot of ribbing because of my background."

Through contacts he made while in the military, Jaracz's first job as a civilian was in the health-care industry for Humana in Louisville, and from there he went to Columbia/HCA. Most recently he has been selling radiology equipment, and no, these are not things he imagined he'd be doing while he was at Kentucky or in the army.

"If anyone had told me in the service I'd be in health care sales, I'd not have thought it possible," Jaracz says. "One thing led to another, and I moved from one thing to the next, and here I am."

"Here" is Crestwood, Kentucky, a small town in southern Oldham County. This is where Jaracz has settled in after two decades of army travel. After being mostly oblivious to the reach of Kentucky basketball while doing the army brat thing, Jaracz's three children have since learned just how significant a role their father plays in Wildcats lore—and just how significant Wildcats lore is in the state of Kentucky.

"Because we traveled a lot, they didn't get an appreciation of what a big deal Kentucky basketball is until we moved to Kentucky," Jaracz says. "Then we came here when they were in elementary and middle school, and we'd go out to places and people would recognize my name. That was a surprise to them, because I was just Daddy."

As legacies go, Jaracz could do a lot worse.

Where Have You Gone?

ROGER NEWMAN

Basketball simply wasn't that important to Roger Newman, a fact that was initially as surprising to Newman as it was to the man who recruited him to Kentucky, legendary coach Adolph Rupp.

Growing up in Greenville, Kentucky, Newman had become a small-town legend thanks to his ability to play basketball. He earned the ultimate prize for a Kentucky kid, a scholarship to play for Rupp's Wildcats, and spent the 1956-57 season averaging 16.1 points for the Kentucky freshman team. Stardom awaited, but after that season Newman left the program (and his scholarship) to concentrate on academics.

He explains his road to self-discovery like so:

"In my home town in Kentucky, if you played basketball, that's all you did in high school," Newman says. "If you were a good athlete—and I was, I could play—then that's really all that you know about yourself and how people feel about you. In college I discovered I liked the academic side of things a great deal.

"After I decided, 'Hey, I don't want to play basketball any more,' it comes as a bit of a shock, because all of the people who had so much of an interest in you no longer have an interest. It's a rather rude awakening, I would say."

By the fall of 1960, Newman was a Kentucky senior who had yet to play a varsity game for Kentucky—but don't tell Newman those were wasted years. He spent that time laying the academic foundation for what became a diverse career in business, first as a city planner, then as a Chicago commodities trader who dabbled in Kentucky farming and Texas cattle.

An interesting man, Roger Newman.

ROGER NEWMAN

Years lettered: 1960-61
Career totals: 397 points, 265 rebounds

In the late 1950s Kentucky fans probably found him more confounding than intriguing. A rugged forward who played bigger than his six-foot-four, 190-pound frame suggested he would, Newman was part of Rupp's star-crossed 1956 recruiting class that saw guard Corky Withrow choose professional baseball over college basketball and forward Jackie Moreland choose Louisiana Tech over Kentucky. Withrow reached the Major Leagues in 1963 with the St. Louis Cardinals—he went hitless in nine career at-bats—while Moreland became a double-figure scorer for the New Orleans Buccaneers of the America Basketball Association.

Unlike Withrow and Moreland, Newman did finally play for Kentucky. He rejoined the program as a fifth-year senior in 1960-61 and finished second on the team in scoring (14.2 points per game) and first in rebounds (9.5). To this day Newman owns the NCAA Tournament record for free throws made in an East Regional game, converting 17 in a 1961 loss to eventual NCAA runner-up Ohio State.

During his three-year layoff from Rupp's program, Newman had stayed in basketball shape by playing for a competitive YMCA team in Lexington that included ex-college players from both Kentucky and Louisville. Their YMCA team played the freshman teams of area colleges, a bit of scheduling trivia that ultimately delayed Newman's Kentucky comeback.

"I was going to join the team in [January] 1960," he says. "I was friends with [assistant coach] Harry Lancaster, and the coaches got word to me that they needed a player. As I recall, Billy Ray Lickert had a calcium deposit on his side and missed [five] games, and I was going to play the second half of that season. I remember, I was going to play the game at Georgia Tech [on January 25, 1960], but the SEC commissioner ruled I couldn't because I had played organized ball that year at the YMCA."

Instead, Newman made his varsity debut the following season after making an unsteady peace with Rupp, who didn't take kindly to basketball players who weren't consumed by basketball. Forgive him, but Newman just wasn't consumed. If his three-year hiatus at Kentucky didn't make that point, his snubbing of the Boston Celtics did. The Celtics were in the middle of their NBA dynasty when they drafted Newman in 1960, but Newman didn't bother showing up at training camp. When the Syracuse Nationals drafted him the following year, it was the same thing.

In fact, Newman's indifference to basketball is such that, to this day, he has his own story wrong. He recalls it was Syracuse that drafted him in 1960, and Boston in 1961. No matter. He wasn't going to play professionally, regardless.

"I think I have maybe a different perspective than most people," he says. "I loved the competition and enjoyed the people I played with, but Bobby

Knight made a statement once that sticks out in my mind. He was talking about sports writers when he said something like, 'By the third grade we've all learned how to read and write, but then most of us go on to something else.' I look at it from the basketball side: When I was growing up, most people would play basketball and then go on to other things. I just went on to other things a little bit earlier than most people."

He would go on to do a lot of other things, but first he went on to get an advanced education. It's ironic, because for a guy whose early days at Kentucky were marked by academic indifference, Newman turned out to be quite the student. After helping the Wildcats to a 19-9 record and NCAA Tournament appearance in 1960-61, Newman won a peculiar academic scholarship from the state of Kentucky.

Back then, Kentucky would pay a student for specialized schooling if the student agreed to spend an equal number of years working for the state. On the state's dime, Newman spent two years at the University of North Carolina in Chapel Hill getting his master's degree in city planning, and then he returned to Kentucky to be a city planner in Hopkinsville. After three years working for the state, Newman went into private business for four years as a city planner before making a radical career change in 1970.

"I had a cousin and a stepfather in the commodities/futures business in Chicago, and they were looking for someone to help," Newman says. "I said, 'Okay, why not?'"

Newman had found his calling. Trading commodities on the floor of the Chicago Mercantile Exchange was a mixture of academics and basketball, a competitive environment that required brains more than brawn. It was a rush, and Newman proved to be quite good at it. He spent his first four or five years working with investors' money, and did well enough to spend the next 25 years investing his own.

Along the way, Newman expanded his personal portfolio. He entered the cattle business in Texas, owning two feed lots, and he bought an 1,110-acre farm in western Kentucky. He sold the feed lots in the late 1990s but he still owns the farm, which has been run for nearly 30 years by a fellow UK graduate.

Newman's love, though, was the floor of the Chicago Mercantile Exchange. He found it intellectually stimulating, exhilarating and humbling, often in the same day.

"It's a money-management situation, and if you do it properly, you are in fact rewarded," Newman says. "But that isn't really the end. Finding out how to get rewarded, even more than the actual reward, is the most fulfilling part.

"But there are bad days. You have to make management decisions throughout the day, and there are times when you think you have everything figured out and rather abruptly you find out you do not. And there's not any advance notice."

Newman has a wife and three children, including a son who would make Bob Knight cringe (he's a sports writer in the Milwaukee area). Factor in his family and his business interests, and Newman hasn't been a regular at the annual functions for former Kentucky basketball players.

Oh, let's be honest: Newman hasn't been to a function in more than two decades.

"After I left Kentucky [in 1970], I was busy," he says. "Raising the family, so forth and so on. If I did go back to Kentucky, it was for the farm. Basketball was a part of my life, but that part has been behind me for years."

Where Have You Gone?

SAUL SMITH

Saul Smith had a schedule, and darn it, he was supposed to keep to that schedule. The former Kentucky point guard was going to be a Division I assistant coach at age 23 or 24. By 30 he hoped to be running his own program, just like his dad at Kentucky. Unlike Tubby Smith, who has shown no interest in professional basketball, Saul Smith's schedule ultimately ended with him coaching in the NBA.

"I had a dream and a plan," he says.

Then Saul got greedy. He never felt he'd play professionally, not so much because he wasn't good enough, but because in his NBA dreams he always wore a sports jacket, not a jersey. But then the Houston Rockets called after his senior season, inviting him to play for their 2001 summer team. Smith was a few classes short of his degree, which he'd need to break into college coaching, but after the Rockets called he made the kind of decision he never made as a solid college point guard.

He abandoned the plan.

"Dad was like, 'You can always finish school. Go and see if this is what you want to do,'" Saul says. "So I tried it. I did love pro basketball, actually."

Smith never made it into the NBA, but he spent two seasons with the Columbus (Georgia) Riverdragons of the NBDL, ranking among league leaders in 2001-02 in three-point shooting at 42.5 percent.

By June 2003, Smith had veered far from his plan. He was 24, not coaching in Division I, not coaching anywhere. Worse, after living for more than a decade with the goal of becoming a coach, he wasn't sure if he wanted to coach any more.

SAUL SMITH

Years lettered: 1997-98, 1998-99, 1999-2000
Career totals: 730 points, 26 rebounds, 363 assists
(ninth in UK history), 152 steals

You can't blame him. At Kentucky he saw the very best of college basketball, including a national championship in 1998, but he also saw the very worst. In those days his father was disliked by a segment of the Kentucky fan base, and Saul was disliked more. He was ridiculed as "Daddy's boy" or even "Daddy's girl" in opposing gyms, and he was booed in Rupp Arena— as a senior—when his father sent him into the Vanderbilt game for freshman Cliff Hawkins. Saul, who had been slumping, responded to the boos with a career-high 18 points.

This has always been one tough kid. At age two he underwent massive surgery to fix a hole in his skull that was leaking spinal fluid. He nearly died, then 11 months later underwent more surgery, this time to have part of his hip fused into his skull. If it weren't for his floppy hair, everyone would see the horrendous scars.

No one can see the scarring he experienced at Kentucky, scarring that could only happen to the point guard/son of the most scrutinized coach in college basketball. He locked it away, sharing his pain only with his mother and older brother, G.G., who had played for their father at Georgia.

"I struggled like any other 18-year-old kid would," Saul says. "I did it mainly in the privacy of my own home. It wasn't in my facial expressions when I was out. Even if I was pissed off or mad, not many people would know it because I wouldn't show it. I got emotional once or twice, but it was rare. I called my mom or my brother with it. I couldn't talk to my dad, not then. We have a great relationship, but it's even better now that I don't play for him. You definitely have to be careful when you approach your coach with certain things, because he might start thinking, 'Should he be leading this team?' I think I held it together pretty well."

That he did. Smith finished his Kentucky career with 110 victories, two SEC Tournament titles and one NCAA ring. He scored 730 points and had 364 assists, ninth in school history.

Two years later, his NBDL playing career finished in the summer of 2003, Smith explored the possibility of law school. No, really—he explored it. This is a big-time planner, remember, so before he committed himself to attending law school, he spent a summer interning for a Lexington law firm.

"I wanted to answer some questions," he says. "Is this what I want to do? Do these people come to work happy? What do they do? They wanted to see if I had what it takes, and I wanted to see what it took. By the end of the summer I figured out [law school] wasn't what I wanted to pursue. I still had some more undergrad [classes] to finish, so I enrolled in school and went on staff with my father, doing what I love."

Saul tracked Kentucky's defensive pressure statistics during the 2003-04 season and worked with Hawkins and Gerald Fitch, more mentally than physically. He knew what it was like to play for his father. Tubby wasn't just hard on Saul. He's hard on all of his players, especially his point guards.

"I was in their ear," Saul says. "Mainly, I was giving lots of encouragement."

Kentucky's 2003-04 season ended March 21 in the NCAA Tournament. One week later Saul Smith turned 25. A short time after that, Tennessee Tech coach Mike Sutton offered a job on his staff.

Tennessee Tech was perfect. Smith had considered playing for the Golden Eagles out of high school before following his father to Kentucky, and Sutton was a former Kentucky assistant.

Sutton liked Smith's bloodlines and playing experience, but he loved Smith's passion, saying he was "impressed by how excited Saul is about the opportunity to coach, and to come to Tennessee Tech."

Sutton hired Smith that July, the heart of the summer evaluation period, and put Smith on the road right away.

"They gave me some pointers, and then I was on the road for about 10 days," Smith says. "They told me, 'We're going to throw you right in the fire.' That's good, that's what I want. I don't mind learning hands on, on the fly."

Even with his unplanned, two-year detour into professional basketball, Saul dreams of being a head coach at age 30, saying, "I might be a year behind schedule, but I can catch up."

Don't bet against him. Smith may be young, but he's smart and meticulous, confident and fearless. He's also motivated by his older brother. G.G. Smith spent the 2002-03 season on Sutton's first staff at Tennessee Tech, then moved to Hawaii to be with his wife, a budding doctor. They've moved to Savannah, where G.G. was hired in 2004 as an assistant at Division II Armstrong Atlantic State.

Whether G.G. knows it or not, the race is on. Saul wants to be a head coach, and he wants to be a head coach first.

"He might not be competing, but I am," Saul says. "I want to do better than him. I just do."

Where Have You Gone?

SCOTTY BAESLER

Of all the basketball players in Kentucky history, no-names and legends and everyone in between, none became a more successful politician than Scotty Baesler. No surprise there. A starting point guard on Kentucky's 1962 and '63 teams featuring Cotton Nash, Baesler led the Wildcats in assists (4.3 per game) one season, led them in foul shooting (85.5 percent) another season, and was Adolph Rupp's captain in 1963. Successful politician, Scotty Baesler? Why not?

Now, about Cuba and the tobacco farm ...

Little bit of a surprise there.

Baesler has held four different public offices, including a decade-long run as mayor of Lexington from 1972-82. He has served as a judge and as a U.S. representative, and in losing bids for governor in 1991 and U.S. senator in 1998, he starred in two of the most expensive elections in state history.

Then he became a tobacco farmer. Strange career move, that one, but Baesler has an honest answer for his decision to leave behind politics for something else—anything else.

"I just didn't want to ask people for money any more," he says, referring to the fund-raising required for runs at major public offices. "I've asked for millions over the years, and it's not fun. After a while, after you've been looking for them to give you money for so long, you can't look people in the eye."

And that's why Scotty Baesler, at age 58, became a tobacco farmer in 1999. Tobacco farming has proved to be a completely different challenge than basketball or politics, games in which the opponent is well-defined and

SCOTTY BAESLER

Years lettered: 1961-62, 1962-63
Career totals: 537 points, 211 rebounds, 158 assists

at least somewhat predictable. In his foray into professional agriculture, Baesler found his No. 1 obstacle had become the weather, which encroaches upon the thin profit margins of any tobacco farmer.

All things considered, though, Baesler would prefer to put up with the vagaries of the weather than stomaching any more of the glad-handing, back-slapping, money-raising ways of a high-profile politician.

"I enjoy farming because you don't have to mess with people," he says. "I did politics for 30 years of my life, and it was fun, but now it's time for something else."

Tobacco farming? That's something else, all right. Baesler describes tobacco season as a ten-month process running from late spring one year to early spring the next. The days are long, running just about from sunrise to sunset.

During the 2004-05 tobacco season, Baesler figures he was going to grow nearly 600,000 pounds over 300 acres, though the land wasn't all his. He leased land from others, going from farm to farm to inquire about the availability of land. A typical lease would see Baesler giving a farmer 65 cents per pound of whatever he could sell from that particular piece of land. To raise tobacco all over the Lexington area, Baesler hires seasonal workers—employing as many as 20 on any given day, depending on the time of year.

"It's very intensive, the labor," Baesler says. "It's not mechanized at all—same as it was about a hundred years ago. You can't mechanize it. It's more efficient with people, but the margins are very thin because of the weather and all the costs involved."

Baesler is accustomed to professional life on the edge. As a mayor and then U.S. representative, he forever lived one public misstep away from political oblivion. Now, in addition to his tobacco farming, he walks the especially delicate line between the United States and Cuba. Baesler walks that line as a go-between for business interests in Kentucky and Cuba.

"I travel to Cuba a lot," he says. "I try to get Americans, particularly Kentuckians, to do business with Cuba. I represent several Kentucky firms, making sure they have the contacts they need. Right now you can sell agricultural products to Cuba under our law, and ultimately you can export and import. I go about four times a year. There's one group of people in Cuba that deals with the United States, and I know them pretty well."

Baesler knows all kinds of interesting folks. During his time on Capitol Hill he got to know scores of politicians simply by playing pickup basketball every afternoon at four in the House of Representatives' gym. He says Steve Largent, a Hall of Fame receiver for the Seattle Seahawks before going into politics, was the best-conditioned athlete in the gym, but that the games were generally good no matter who showed up.

"Talent, age and conditioning are the three leveling factors," says Baesler, who at Kentucky averaged 10.9 points in 1962 and 9.7 in 1963. "I was one of the better ones, but there were a whole lot of good ones. Playing every day at four ... that's the most fun you have up there."

Baesler's wife, Alice, also is a recovering politician. She served as a ranking aide in Kentucky's Agriculture Department but lost the 2003 election for state agriculture commissioner. In a strange-but-true twist, Scotty Baesler's wife lost to another ex-Kentucky guard, Richie Farmer, who starred in 1992 for Rick Pitino's "Unforgettables," a team that reached the Elite Eight of the NCAA Tournament.

To no surprise, Scotty Baesler's loyalty to his wife runs deeper than his loyalty to another ex-Wildcat, in this case Farmer. Baesler knows a little bit about what it takes to get a job in agriculture and politics, and he thinks his wife was the right person for the job.

He also knows a little—maybe more than a little—about a lot of other areas of employment. But, what comes next? Nobody knows, and that includes Baesler.

"We'll see what happens," he says. "You never know, never know, I might develop some property. I might do this, might do that. I'm not dead. I might just get out of the farming business and enjoy myself."

Where Have You Gone?

LINVILLE PUCKETT

Would he have been another Kentucky All-American? Maybe, maybe not. Because there is a question but not an answer, Linville Puckett remains—more than 50 years after he started on the Wildcats' perfect team of 1954—an unsolved mystery in Kentucky basketball lore.

He doesn't remain bitter over his abrupt, midseason departure in 1955. Well, not more than a little. We'll get to that in a minute.

Puckett retired in December 2003 from the Kentucky Department of Transportation, where he worked in vehicle registration, and now he gives his time to his wife and their three children and four grandchildren. His family boards horses, and one of his sons is remodeling a home. All of that keeps Puckett busy. Too busy, he jokes.

"I told my wife I'd rather go back to work," Puckett says. "It wasn't as hard when I was working."

Looking back at his days at Kentucky? That can be hard. Puckett was a basketball hero at Clark County High, leading legendary coach Letcher Norton's 1951 team to a state championship. Puckett scored 47 points in a Sweet 16 tournament game, breaking future Kentucky teammate Cliff Hagan's record of 41. Going to Kentucky, starring for Kentucky, was the next logical step for Puckett.

He did go to Kentucky, and he did play for Adolph Rupp, but he never became the star he could have been. Nighttime was his favorite time, and while Rupp wanted his boys in bed, Puckett preferred a place called The Palms. It was a bar.

"I never played hung over," he says. "But I liked my beer—yeah."

Photo courtesy of Linville Puckett

LINVILLE PUCKETT

Years lettered: 1953-54
Career totals: 259 points

Rupp didn't like that, or so the party line goes. Before the Wildcats' February 3, 1955 game against Florida, Rupp announced that Puckett, a junior guard, had been dismissed from the team for missing practice. Over the years, the unofficial stance emanating from Kentucky has been that the partying Puckett was too much of a free spirit for Rupp, thus his dismissal.

That might be true, though Puckett disagrees with the notion that his dismissal was Rupp's idea. Puckett says he walked away from the program after a dispute with teammates.

"I left," is how Puckett starts the story. "It wasn't a problem with Adolph and me as much as [with] the team. We had a rule: If you left town, you were supposed to ask Coach if you could go home. I just lived 16 miles away in Winchester, so I was going home all the time. One weekend all the boys went home except for Bill Evans and me. When they came back, I was sitting at a service station. They said, 'Coach Rupp found out we left, and he's going to take our $15 laundry money. Would you say you went home, too?'

"See, they were all afraid of Coach Rupp, but he never bothered me; I had a coach in high school as tough as him, Letcher Norton. So I said yeah, and I told [Rupp] I went, too. Someone [on the team] said, 'Well, if they take our money, we'll all just quit.' I said, 'If that's what everybody's going to do, that's what we'll do.' We had a meeting, and sure enough, [Rupp] told us he'd take our money."

That's where Puckett says his career unraveled. He says his teammates didn't, in fact, threaten to quit. Instead, Puckett says, some of them gave the coaching staff a variety of excuses for their unexcused absence.

"They said, 'My mother's sick,' or, 'My grandmother's sick,'" Puckett says. "I told the coaches I went out of town, too, but I just didn't have a reason. After that, Coach said, 'The ones that want to stay, go on and practice. The ones that don't can go out the door.'

"They went on the court, and I went out the door. I didn't want to play with guys like that. I was the only one not guilty."

And so ended the career of a player good enough to start as a sophomore on Kentucky's 25-0 team of 1953-54, perhaps the most dominant team in program history. The Wildcats' average margin of victory that season was 27.2 points per game, with only two opponents keeping within single digits. Puckett, a six-foot shooting guard, averaged 5.1 points on that team, then averaged 9.7 per game in 1954-55 before leaving the program.

To this day Puckett insists his split had little to do with Rupp, and that his only beef with the Baron lies in the loss of his retired jersey. After that perfect season of 1953-54, which saw the Wildcats not go to the NCAA Tournament because of the ineligibility of stars Cliff Hagan, Frank Ramsey and Lou Tsioropoulos, Rupp retired the starters' jerseys, hanging them in the rafters. When Puckett left the program, Rupp removed Puckett's No. 33 from the rafters.

"He took it back," Puckett says. "I don't think you should do that."

Still, Puckett talks about his days at Kentucky and beyond with fondness. He played one season at Kentucky Wesleyan as a transfer and probably had a future in the NBA, but the NBA wasn't paying much in those days so he quit the game to become part-owner of his old campus hangout, The Palms. Puckett didn't have any money for that business venture, but he says he didn't need any money. The Palms' owner wanted the gregarious Puckett badly enough to give him a percentage without a down payment. Six months later the owner died, and within two years Puckett was the principal owner. He was 24.

Puckett proved to be quite the businessman, luring big-time acts to his place for weeknight showings. Puckett says he would get Conway Twitty or Jerry Lee Lewis or whomever to swing through town on their way north from Nashville.

"I was about the first one around here that started big-time music during the week," he says. "I was giving them $500 a night. That was big money then, too. I put a $5 cover charge on the door, and the lounge I had, it was packed every night. That was about the best time of my life."

Puckett says he sold the property to the American Legion in 1971, then dabbled in different things—working for a nephew's fencing company, running his own fertilizer-spreading company—before spending nearly 20 years with the Department of Transportation.

Even though his jersey no longer hangs in the rafters and his name isn't in the official team photo from that ill-fated 1954-55 season, Puckett says Kentucky Nation hasn't forgotten him.

"I get recognized everywhere I go," he says. "I think it's because of the way I left."

Trailed by question marks.

Where Have You Gone?

ANTHONY EPPS

The phone was going to ring. The NBA break was going to come. Anthony Epps knew that, could feel it in his bones just as surely as he knew four years earlier that Kentucky was the place for him—even though Kentucky wasn't offering a scholarship.

That part of his basketball life turned out all right. Although Epps was prepared to walk on to Kentucky, a scholarship became available in 1993 and was presented to him. Soon he was embarking on a career that saw him play in 141 games—more than all but four players in school history—and start at point guard in the Wildcats' victory in the 1996 national championship game against Syracuse.

So there he was in 1997, waiting for the phone to ring. Waiting for his NBA break. It would come. It had to.

Didn't it?

"Nope," Epps says today, rueful but not bitter. "I never got my break out of college."

Typical. Epps was the ultimate team player for the ultimate college basketball team of the 1990s, Rick Pitino's massive collection of future NBA talent that ran roughshod over the rest of America. Kentucky went 34-2 in 1995-96 and was getting even better at the end, when the Wildcats won their six 1996 NCAA Tournament games by an average margin of 22 points.

Nine players from that team would play in the NBA. Anthony Epps, probably the team's most indispensable player, was not among them.

"I sacrificed a lot," he says. "I didn't score all that much because my role was to get other people the ball."

ANTHONY EPPS

Years lettered: 1993-94, 1994-95, 1995-96, 1996-97
Career totals: 881 points, 329 rebounds, 544 assists (second in UK history), 155 three-pointers (fifth in UK history)

There was honor in that, and certainly there was success. Epps has a championship ring from his junior season of 1995-96. But there was not a phone call from the NBA.

If professional basketball wasn't going to pursue Epps, well, he was going to pursue professional basketball. His pursuit took him not only to North Dakota (Fargo of the International Basketball Association) but to South Dakota as well (Sioux Falls, Continental Basketball Association). Epps's basketball odyssey also took him to Trenton of the International Basketball League and Louisville of the United Pro Basketball League.

The IBA, CBA, IBL and UPBL—that's a lot of initials right there. None of them, of course, added up to the initials Epps most desired.

By late 2004, Epps had long since come to grips with the fact that an NBA career wasn't going to happen. In fact, by 2004 he thought he was finished playing professionally for any league. His last professional experience had come in 2003 in the UPBL, a four-team league that had some decent ex-college players mixed in with guys from schools like Bellarmine, Northwestern State and Wisconsin-Superior. Epps was a star in that league, leading Louisville to the UPBL championship and winning Most Valuable Player honors in the postseason tournament.

When the season ended and the UPBL disbanded, Epps thought he was done. He cut ties with his basketball agency, Global Sports Plaza of Macedonia. His phone, he knew, was not going to ring.

"It was time to get on with my life," Epps says.

But basketball wasn't finished with him just yet. In 2004, the World Basketball Association formed. Epps was curious.

Later that year the WBA placed a franchise in his hometown, Louisville. Epps was more than curious. He attended a tryout and easily earned a spot on the team. By the fall of 2004, he was eagerly awaiting another season in the professional basketball wilderness.

"I've got a burning desire," he says. "I love the game—basketball is me. Sports in general, I'm just a competitive person. And now as I get older, I realize winning's not everything as long as you can go out there and compete and look yourself in the mirror and know you gave it your all."

Epps has taken that same zeal into his life away from basketball. Well, somewhat away from basketball. About the time he realized his NBA dreams weren't going to come true, Epps took a job as a youth director at the Kentuckiana Boys & Girls Clubs in Jeffersonville, Indiana, just across the Indiana border from Louisville.

Epps was drawn to that kind of work because he knew most of the kids roaming around that small gym in Kentuckiana had been just like him once—a kid from a broken home.

"I love working with kids," he says. "I feel like I can give a lot back to them because I grew up the same way a lot of them did, in single-parent homes. I've had success growing up that way, and I try to show them they can do it, too."

For Epps, the vehicle to success was athletics. He was an all-state football player at Marion County High School in Lebanon, Kentucky, but basketball was his first love—and Kentucky was his only love. That's why he already had decided to play for the Wildcats even before a happy combination of events (junior Jamal Mashburn's departure for the 1993 NBA Draft, and Charles O'Bannon's decision to attend UCLA instead of Kentucky) freed up the scholarship that Kentucky coach Rick Pitino would give to Epps.

Epps finished ranked among Kentucky's all-time leaders in assists (second with 544) and steals (sixth, 184), and also scored 881 points. His career can best be summed up by the 1996 NCAA title game, when Kentucky defeated Syracuse 76-67. Epps handed out seven assists and committed just one turnover. He played all 40 minutes.

He never scored.

Yes, while Epps won a lot in college, he sacrificed a lot of himself to do it. Maybe that's why he refuses to let the game go, spending his free moments at the small Kentuckiana gym working on his game and preparing for the 2004 WBA season. Or, maybe it's something even more basic than that.

Maybe Epps, even at age 29 and with three kids of his own, simply loves the game too much to give it up. Not yet.

"I've got at least three years left in me," he said in late 2004. "Maybe four."

Where Have You Gone?

JERRY BIRD

L ife happened to Jerry Bird, but life didn't change him. He arrived at Kentucky almost unbelievably humble, became a scrub on the basketball team, then a star. He was drafted and served in the U.S. Army. He was drafted and played in the NBA. After retiring he got one great job, then another. He still gets recognized to this day.

And to this day, he's unbelievably humble.

"I didn't come across as cocky or anything," he wants to know, "did I?"

That's how Bird ended a lengthy interview for this book, speaking by phone from his home in Corbin, Kentucky And the answer to your question, Jerry, is simple. No, you did not come across as cocky—or anything.

Jerry Bird, thinking he's better than anyone else? Please. On the weekend of this interview, it took several attempts to reach Bird because he was at the local cemetery in Corbin. He wasn't attending a funeral or visiting a grave. He was helping a friend clean the place.

"I just went over there to mow a little," Bird says.

Maybe more than a little. Bird has this habit of downplaying his finest moments. Within the state borders he is a well-known face and name, nearly a half-century after he averaged 16.2 points and 11.3 rebounds as a Kentucky senior in 1955-56. Elsewhere, Bird is routinely greeted by strangers who take note of his looming 6-foot-6, 215-pound build and ask him, "Did you play basketball?"

Bird answers them like so:

"Yeah, I tried."

Isn't that a hoot? He tried! Sure he tried. Bird tried so hard that his No. 22 jersey was given a place of honor in the rafters of Rupp Arena.

JERRY BIRD
(RIGHT)

Years lettered: 1953-54, 1954-55, 1955-56
Honors: retired jersey No. 22
Career totals: 713 points, 589 rebounds

But that's what you get from Bird, all these years later, about his days at Kentucky. It's about what you get from Bird when he talks about his career after Kentucky, too. Here's what he says when asked about the years from 1956 to 2000:

"I spent two years in the service, played a little pro ball. Took a job with Phillips Petroleum Company for ten years, then [spent] 30 years with the American Greetings Corporation."

That's it?

"I worked in human resources," he says. "Then I retired."

End of story.

Well ...

See, if you dig just a bit deeper, you learn the moral of Bird's story: Good things happen to good people. You won't learn that from Bird, of course. Does he call himself good? No way. He's too worried about coming off negatively to realize his impact is just the opposite. The two are probably related, come to think of it.

But the part about good things and good people, that's true with Bird. It was true at Kentucky, where he was a reserve on the Wildcats' undefeated team in 1953-54, and a star on their teams in 1955 and '56 that went a combined 43-9. It was true during his role in the American conflict with Korea, which already had ended when he was drafted in August 1956. His service was to stay in the United States and play on the Army's basketball team.

And it was especially true after Bird returned from service and entered the work force. He took a job with Phillips Petroleum, which sent him to Indianapolis for training before assigning him a territory to work. At the end of his training, a Phillips manager called Bird into his office and apologized for the inconvenience, but told him the company was going to send him to ... Corbin, Kentucky.

"They didn't know I was from Corbin," Bird says. "They just thought I was from Lexington. When they said I was going to Corbin, I couldn't believe it. My wife and I bought a home here, and we've lived almost 40 years in this house."

That's what you call a happy coincidence, but happy coincidences seem to be the norm for Bird. Good things, good people—remember?

At Corbin High, which he helped lead to a third-place finish in the 1950 state basketball tournament, Bird's teammates included Frank Selvy—who went on to make headlines at Furman University in Greenville, South Carolina, when he scored 100 points against Newberry on February 13, 1954. A few years later, after Bird had finished his service with the U.S. Army, he signed a contract with the New York Knicks. He had been drafted in 1956 by Minneapolis, but the army got him first, so the Knicks waited until 1958 to claim his rights. Pro basketball was a goal, but the Knicks? Bird was a small-town guy to the core, and he wasn't sure about New York until he arrived and learned one of his teammates would be Selvy.

Another teammate at Corbin High, Roy Kidd, went on to become a hall of fame football coach at Eastern Kentucky. Kidd retired after the 2002 season as the sixth-winningest coach in Division I or I-AA history, with national championships in 1979 and '82. Kidd's best player on that 1982 team was an All-American receiver named Steve Bird—Jerry's son. Steve Bird became a football coach himself, coaching receivers at West Virginia in 2004.

Football is in the Bird blood, even if Jerry, the oldest of four brothers, played basketball. The next three Birds who came along—younger brothers Calvin, Rodger and Billy—played football for Kentucky. Calvin and Rodger were drafted by NFL teams, while Billy was inducted into the Kentucky High School Athletic Association's Hall of Fame.

Beyond high school, Jerry Bird's only brush with organized football was during his stint in the military, when he was a manager for the Army football team. Bird also played baseball in the army, though he dismisses his baseball talent by saying, "I was just an ordinary baseball player."

Maybe he was, but to take Bird's word for it would be foolishness. He is, after all, a minimalist. When asked for his single-game scoring high at Kentucky, Bird said he didn't know. Pushed, he admitted to scoring in the 30s once, but said he didn't remember the exact total. Pushed further, he wouldn't give the exact number.

We looked it up: 34. That's the damage Bird incurred against Dayton's Bill Uhl, a seven-footer who scored 1,627 career points for the Flyers. Bird's career day came during his senior season, when regular Kentucky center Bob Burrow was out with a sprained ankle. Bird moved to the pivot for one game, and in words he would appreciate, he did okay.

Where Have You Gone?

RICK
ROBEY

If he weren't so darned likable, it would be awfully easy not to like Rick Robey.

In high school he won a state championship. At Kentucky he won an NCAA title. With the Boston Celtics he won an NBA title. With the United States he won a gold medal. Now, as a realtor in Louisville, he has become the top agent in his state and one of the most successful agents (gulp) in the world. He owns a winter home on the beach in Destin, Florida, and hopes to retire there in his early 50s. Alongside him will be his lovely wife, Bonnie, owner of a thriving mortgage company.

A guy like Rick Robey, a winner in almost everything he has done, could make the rest of us angry. But then he opens his mouth, and all is forgiven.

"You know how they say it's better to be lucky than good?" he asks. "I've been awfully lucky."

He's lying—Robey has been considerably more "good" than "lucky"—but that's okay. Humility is a fine thing, and in Robey's case the humility has been earned. After injuries ended his NBA career in 1986, Robey took a big chunk of his savings and invested heavily in a restaurant.

Oops.

"I failed at it," he says. "I failed at it and I didn't like it, and the lesson I learned was that if you're going to live something, live something that you enjoy. (The restaurant business) was the wrong industry for me. What I'm doing now, I love. I wake up every morning and look forward to it."

After getting out of the restaurant business, Robey acquired his real estate license in 1989 and, as he puts it, "piddled around for five or six years" before getting serious. Getting serious coincided with moving from

176

RICK ROBEY

Years lettered: 1974-75, 1975-76, 1976-77, 1977-78
Honors: All-SEC and All-American, 1976-77, 1977-78;
retired jersey No. 53
Career totals: 1,395 points (19th in UK history), 838 rebounds
(eighth in UK history), 146 assists

Lexington to Louisville, where he and his wife had a growing number of friends. Robey says he spent his first two or three years in Louisville learning the area, laying the foundation for the empire he currently oversees. His team, Robey-Malone-Farrar, was RE/MAX's top-selling team in 2003 in the Kentucky-Indiana region, and broke into the company's international top 100. The team also finished 2003 ranked No. 1 among realty teams in Kentucky, regardless of their company.

"I am fulfilled," he says. "I enjoy being around people, meeting people. It's a people's business, selling real estate, plus it's not something where you have to go sit behind a desk from eight to five. You're out showing properties or listing properties. You're involved with the community."

Being named Rick Robey in the state of Kentucky? Yeah, that helps. But Robey says his business would suffer, not thrive, if he relied on nothing more than name recognition.

"It gets you in the door, but when you're dealing with someone's biggest investment, whether you're named Rick Robey or not you need to get them top dollar for their house," he says. "Yes, my name does open doors—but after that door is open, you need to do the job."

In another life, his life as a basketball player, Robey spent almost 15 years making his name recognizable all over the country. It began in New Orleans, where he led Brother Martin High School to the state championship and was named Louisiana's Mr. Basketball as a senior in 1974.

The six-foot-10 Robey arrived at Kentucky with another freshman big man, 6-10 Mike Phillips, and immediately they were dubbed the "twin towers." As a freshman Robey supplanted senior Bob Guyette as the team's top inside threat, and the Wildcats improved from 13-13 the previous season to 26-5. By the time he finished Kentucky had gone 102-21 in four seasons, and Robey had added the 1978 national championship ring to his 1974 Louisiana state title.

Robey also had a gold medal as a member of the United States' victorious team at the 1975 Pan-American Games in Mexico City. He probably could have had an Olympic gold medal as well, but before tryouts for that 1976 team Robey suffered a hand injury and had to have his tonsils removed. Coupling the medical hassles with his dislike for U.S. coach Dean Smith, with whom Robey says he had had a run-in during a college game in December 1975, Robey turned down in invitation to camp.

"In my basketball career," he says, "that's probably the only regret I have."

Certainly his NBA career was a success, though it ended prematurely. Robey's sophomore season at Kentucky had been derailed by injuries, a hint of things to come at the next level. First, though, came the glory: He was drafted No. 3 overall by the Indiana Pacers in 1978, three spots ahead of future Boston teammate Larry Bird (whom the Celtics picked sixth even though Bird would spend one more season at Indiana State). After averaging 10.4 points and 6.5 rebounds as a rookie with the Pacers, Robey was traded to the Celtics before the 1979-80 season. Two years later the Celtics won the NBA title, with Robey averaging nine points and 4.8 rebounds on a team that also included frontcourt stars like Bird, Robert Parish, Cedric Maxwell and Kevin McHale.

Injuries to his knee and Achilles' began taking their toll on Robey, whose production dwindled until his retirement after the 1986 season.

"I just couldn't run any more," he says. "The wear and tear ... it was just a matter of too many miles. My strength was being able to run up and down the floor, but once my wheels were gone, I was gone."

Five surgeries on his knee and one on his Achilles' eventually eroded his hip, which had to be replaced in the mid-1990s. Still, Robey stays as active as he can, playing golf and dashing around Louisville hunting for antiques when he's not working.

Of course, it seems like he's always working. Ask Bonnie for the best time to reach her husband without disrupting his work, and she'll say—quite seriously—to call him at home some time before 10 p.m. Reach Robey in his office, and phones constantly ring in the background.

"You leave early and get home late, but it's a fun job and I really enjoy it," Robey says. "We both work hard. Bonnie started her mortgage company, Liberty Mortgage, from scratch and has built it up over nine years. She gets some of our loans, but it's not like her office is next to ours. She's done it on her own.

"In four or five years we hope to slow it down and enjoy our hard labors."

You'll be able to find Robey in Florida, living in his three-bedroom, three-bathroom condominium overlooking Destin's white beach. He'll be the 6-10 guy with the huge smile.

Where Have You Gone?

JEFF
SHEPPARD

For the longest time, Jeff Sheppard's life was one for the books—storybooks.

As a sixth-grader in Peachtree City, Georgia, he vowed in a school essay to play basketball for the Kentucky Wildcats and to reach the Final Four. Seven years later, after becoming Georgia's Mr. Basketball as well as a state track champion in the high jump, he was in Rupp Arena wearing No. 15. By the time he graduated he had two national championship rings and one wedding ring, courtesy of his marriage to former Kentucky women's star Stacey Reed, who ranks fifth all-time among the lady Wildcats with 1,482 points. By age 23, Sheppard had even been the subject of a book. Its title: *Heart of a Champion.*

He was a walking, talking superhero.

But, not long ago, Sheppard turned in his cape. The fairy tale is finished, but in its place is something just as pleasurable. Jeff Sheppard now lives a life straight out of a Norman Rockwell painting.

"Wife, two kids, house," Sheppard says. "Yeah, I've got it good."

It could have been different. Better? Worse? Who knows—but different it could have been.

Sheppard lives in London, Kentucky, but he could have been living in London, England. Or Rome, Italy. Or Paris. Name a cool city in Europe, and Sheppard probably could be there right now, earning a handsome salary playing basketball for a living.

Maybe he'd even be back in the NBA. Sheppard spent part of the 1998-99 season with the Atlanta Hawks, scoring 40 points in 18 games. He had subsequent tryouts with the Toronto Raptors in 2000 and the Washington

JEFF SHEPPARD

Years lettered: 1993-94, 1994-95, 1995-96, 1997-98
Career totals: 1,091 points (39th in UK history), 320 rebounds,
288 assists, 125 steals

Wizards in 2001, but always he was among the last players cut. Always, there was a roster spot awaiting him overseas, and Sheppard chose to play in Italy. Along the way he rocked the Italian League's world by winning a lawsuit that allowed Italian teams to have more than two Americans on a roster. Sheppard used that legal victory to land a spot with the Italian club Roseto.

Maybe he'd still be there if it weren't for September 11, 2001. That of course was the day terrorists struck the United States by turning our own commercial airplanes into weapons of mass destruction. At the time Sheppard was in Italy, playing his third season there.

Back in Kentucky, Stacey had just given birth to their first child, a daughter they named Madison. In two months Stacey was set to fly to Italy, where she and Madison were going to live with Jeff. Stacey's parents also were going to make that trip for a visit.

"We bought the tickets and everything," Sheppard says. "They were going to come over in November, and then September 11 happened and changed everything."

Stacey didn't want to fly. Jeff didn't blame her. They were indeed a family again in November of that year, but not in Rome. Sheppard had left his Italian team to come home and be with his wife and daughter. In the ensuing months Sheppard had several offers to return overseas and resume his playing career, but he had made his decision. It was time to get on with the rest of his life.

"I feel great about it," says Sheppard, whose son, Reed, was born in June 2004. "I miss basketball a lot, I'm still healthy, and I can still play. I hated ending my career short over there because I was in a good position, on a great team in Rome in a really good league, and I was starting to get established as a player over there. Things were really looking good, but that's fine.

"I just decided I didn't want to play minor-league basketball anymore. I knew I could do more in this state for my future than playing minor league basketball, and I felt like I had given the NBA a pretty good shot. I almost made it, but it didn't work out. So we just started our life."

The first move was a conversation with Kentucky coach Tubby Smith, who had replaced Rick Pitino in 1997, before Sheppard's final season with the Wildcats. Sheppard was contemplating getting into the coaching business, but he decided instead to pursue a career in business.

The truth is, Sheppard was one of the most popular players in school history, and his legend has only grown since he left. There is money to be made from such fame, and there are lives to be touched. Sheppard wanted to go into a business that would allow him to accomplish both goals. As for his widespread popularity, Sheppard has an idea why it has happened this way.

"What helps is that [in 1998] we were the last team to win a championship at Kentucky," he says. "The way we went out really helps. Everybody remembers us as a winner, and that's great. They remember the last run we had through the NCAA tournament and that's how we finished our career. Not many college athletes can say they finished their college career with a win. That's how people remember me."

That's part of it, but there's more. Sheppard was a pleasing player to watch, a sky-walking shooting guard who once high-jumped seven feet in high school. He used that elevation for dunks as well as his picturesque jump shot.

Then there was his attitude. Even before the 1998 NCAA Tournament—even before the 1998 season began—Sheppard had earned much favor among Kentucky fans by delaying what should have been his senior season for the good of the team. With almost everyone coming back from Kentucky's 1996 national champions, Pitino asked Sheppard to redshirt the 1997 season. Sheppard said okay.

Sheppard already had carved out a niche for himself as an unusually unselfish player. He started 27 games as a sophomore in 1995, but as Pitino's stockpile of future NBA talent grew, Sheppard's playing time shrunk. Although Sheppard's shooting percentages rose to 52 percent overall and 50 percent on three-pointers, his playing time was cut nearly in half in 1996. The Wildcats won a national championship behind Antoine Walker, Ron Mercer and Derek Anderson, and Sheppard never complained about going from starter to ninth man.

After redshirting the 1997 season, in which the Wildcats reached the NCAA title game against Arizona, Sheppard returned to action in 1998. He was a team leader, in production (a team-high 13.7 points per game) and other areas, and the Wildcats won their second national championship in three seasons.

Long story short ... Jeff Sheppard, state hero.

Still, after returning to Kentucky from Italy in November 2001, Sheppard needed a bridge to get him from basketball retirement to entrepreneur-ship. That bridge was Bristol-Myers, where he worked for 18 months in pharmaceutical sales. About a year into his time with Bristol-Myers, Sheppard created a company he called 15Inc., which he used as a launching pad for such activities as motivational speaking, basketball camps and licensed Kentucky apparel sales. After six months, Sheppard was ready to leave Bristol-Myers and turn 15Inc. into a full-time business.

"I just knew in college that I wanted to win, and that mentality is still [with me] ... it's just me," Sheppard says. "I wanted to be the best player individually, I wanted to be on the best team, and I wanted our team to win championships. I still have that mentality. My passion has moved from basketball to trying to be the best salesman and business owner I can be—having the best team surround me—and help other businesses succeed and to do better through the motivational speaking."

Sheppard has all kinds of promotional irons in the fire, including school fundraisers featuring the 15Inc. line of Kentucky sports apparel, but he is kept busiest by his Dream Shapers Tour. In the 2003-04 school year he gave motivational speeches at 72 schools, putting 52,000 miles on his new truck in just eight months, and he set 300 schools as his goal for 2004-05. His mantra: If you want to be it, first you have to dream it.

Sheppard is a walking advertisement for his Dream Shapers Tour. He really did write that paper in sixth grade predicting he'd play in the Final Four for Kentucky. He also vowed in that paper to play in the NBA, another mission he accomplished. Combine his popularity in Kentucky with his ambition to reach as many kids as possible, and he's not just dreaming when he says he wants his Dream Shapers Tour to make a positive impact throughout the state.

"I'm from Georgia, but the state of Kentucky has adopted me," Sheppard says. "It's been a dream come true."